DEATH VALLEY: THE HUNDRED-YEAR BLOOM

by

Holly Cannon

Photography by
Mark Grieco

The Valley of Extremes

On a summer day in 1913, in a month that had already seen five consecutive days of temperatures over 129 degrees, Death Valley hit a mark of 134 degrees, at that time the hottest ever recorded on Earth. Oscar Denton, the caretaker who monitored the weather station at the valley's Greenland Ranch, later said that on that day "(i)t was so hot that swallows in full flight fell to the earth dead. When I went out to read the thermometer with a wet Turkish towel on my head, it was dry before I returned."

Two years later, Fred Corkill, the respected superintendent of the Pacific Coast Borax Company, corroborated the account. "I remember the day very distinctly, as a man by the name of Busch perished in the valley north of the ranch … on account of the heat," he said. "The chauffeur who was with Mr. Busch at the time he perished also very nearly lost his life. I saw him a few days later and he said that a terrific wind prevailed in the valley on that day."

That wind, superheated air that turns the valley into a kiln, is part of a microclimate that makes Death Valley the hottest and driest spot in North America. Its human history, a "gruesome story of a rugged country," has given it a rightly earned reputation for hardship, danger and death.

It was famously christened in 1850 by pioneers attempting to find a shorter route from Utah to the California gold fields. Several died, and the rest nearly perished from thirst and starvation. When the region was extensively mapped by Lt. George Wheeler in 1871 as part of a U.S. government survey, a guide for the expedition reportedly died within hours when ordered to cross the valley on foot. Prospectors who came to Death Valley in the 1860s and '70s in search of gold and silver told stories about finding skeletons without graves and men falling dead with canteens still in their hands. Its "dreaded terrors of heat and dryness" and its oppressive silence were believed to induce insanity.

The valley's aridity is a result of its geography and an ancient climate change. Hundreds of millions of years ago, the area that became the valley was part of a warm sea that receded when tectonic plate movement pushed the land up. As the plates continued to move, the Earth's crust was compressed, causing faulting and the formation of

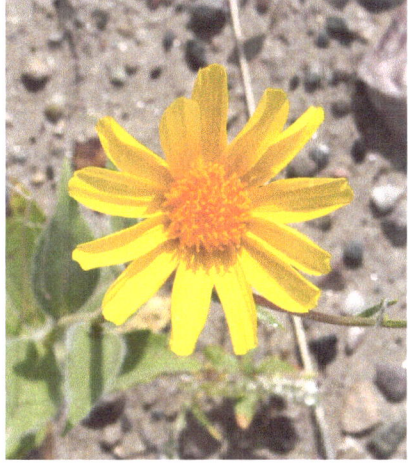

DESERT GOLD
Despite its harsh conditions, Death Valley is home to approximately 1,000 native plant species, of which 50 or more are endemic.

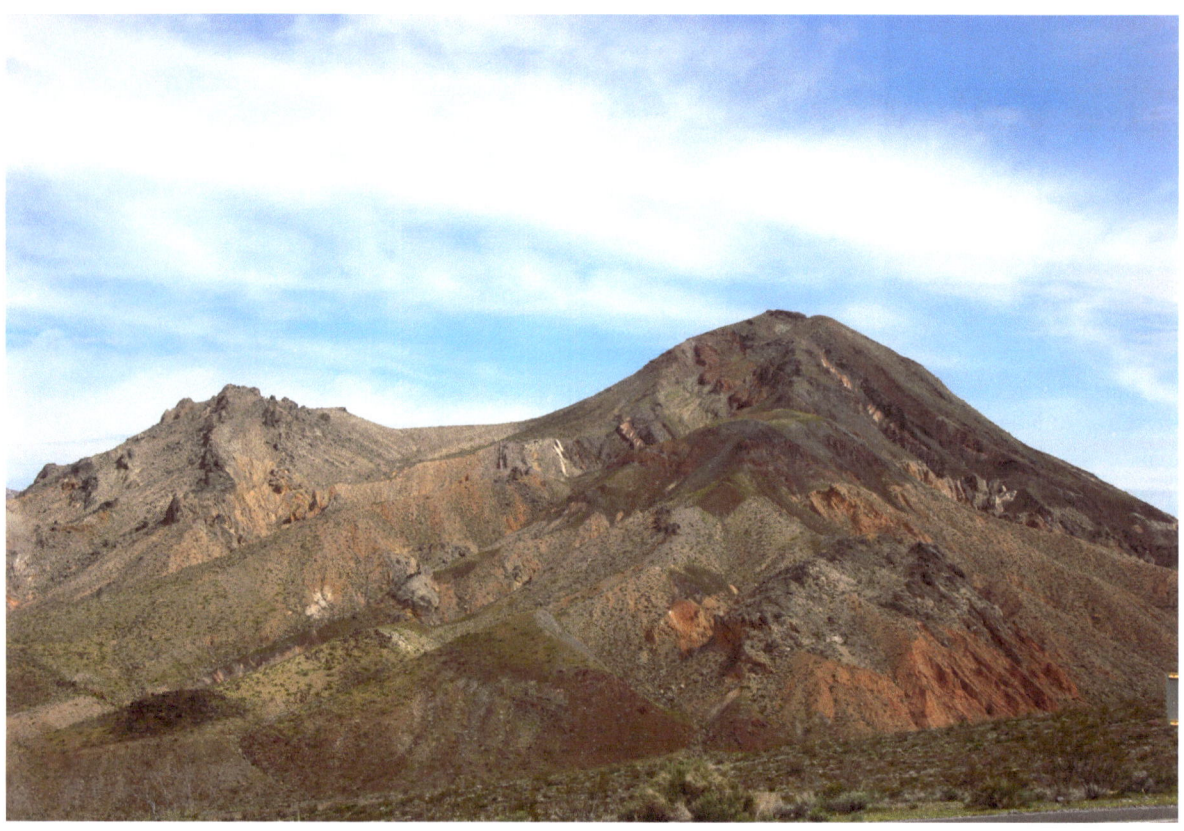

THE COLORS OF RUST
Death Valley's reds, oranges and browns result mainly from the minerals hematite, a red iron oxide, and limonite, a yellow iron oxide.

mountains ranges. As the land surface stretched and cracked, volcanoes erupted, leaving ash and borate mineral deposits behind.

Approximately three million years ago, the plate motion changed, pulling the crust apart instead of pushing it together. Blocks of land slid along the plates, creating alternating mountain ranges and valleys, including the Amargosa and the Panamint ranges with Death Valley between them. During the glacial Pleistocene era between 2.5 million and 12,000 years ago, the valley became part of a group of lakes, collectively known now as Lake Manly. When the climate began to warm and become drier, the lakes evaporated, leaving massive salt pans behind.

As a result, Death Valley is now a north-south basin about 75 miles long and 15 miles wide. Its lowest point, Badwater, lies 282 feet below sea level, the lowest point in North America. Remarkably, just a few miles to the west is the Panamint Range and lofty Telescope Peak, reaching 11,902 feet high. To the east is the steep Amargosa Range that lies close to the Nevada line. Between the two, Death Valley lies in a rain shadow that leaves it in perpetual drought.

Lower elevations generally have warmer ground temperatures, and Death Valley is no exception. In summer, the valley floor, rocky and lacking much plant cover, absorbs sunlight and heats the ground to a high temperature. The air rises up the mountains on either side, and then is pushed down by the atmospheric pressure, where it is reheated near the ground before rising again. In this way, the mountains effectively trap and recirculate hot air, forming the superheated winds that blanket the valley.

In winter, temperatures can fall to freezing, and rain in the mountains can cause flash flooding severe enough to destroy paved roads and buildings. Water, boulders and debris flow freely into the valley and deposit silt and minerals in mile-wide alluvial fans.

In an average year, rainfall in and around Death Valley is usually between one and two inches, although two years have been recorded with no rainfall at all. It's enough water to support a diverse wildlife population, like the chuckwalla lizard, and at higher and cooler elevations, desert bighorn sheep. The valley's kangaroo rat can go for many months without drinking water, while the chuckwalla absorbs water from eating plants and can survive without ever drinking it.

At the lower elevations, vegetation is sparse. Among the most common plants are the creosote bush, which survives by storing water in its leaves for long periods of time, and the mesquite, whose roots tap into underground springs. Both lie low to the ground and don't provide much in the way of shelter or shade.

In the winter of 2004 and the early spring of 2005, a sub-tropical jet stream nicknamed the "Pineapple Express" moved in from Hawaii and unleashed a near-record amount of rain and snow on California. Southern California had 38 inches of rain, more than twice its annual average, and 10 feet of snow fell on the Sierra Nevada within a matter of days. The Mojave Desert received so much rain that it accumulated 119% of its annual average in six months. Death Valley received between five and six inches of rain, or three to four times its annual average.

"In 1891 the weather bureau sent an observer to remain there and take observations during the summer months. When he returned before the expiration of his time, he said he would take 'hell straight' next time."

—D.A. Hufford
Death Valley; Swamper Ike's Traditional Lore: Why, When, How?

It began inauspiciously in August, 2004, when one night of extremely hard rainfall caused flash flooding that killed two people near Furnace Creek. Highway 190, the main north-south road through Death Valley National Park, was partly washed out, and park visitors were evacuated. Over the next eight months, rain fell, by the valley's standards, abundantly.

The result was miraculous. Seeds that had lain dormant for years, or even decades, sprouted. The valley was transformed into a lush landscape of milkweed, gravel ghost, chicory, Fremont phacelia, desert five spots, primrose and an unlikely blanket of dazzling yellow desert gold. The bloom attracted bees and other insects, which in turn attracted birds and other animals.

Botanists and biologists, stunned at the sudden abundance of flora and fauna, raced to Death Valley to document the few short weeks of spring renewal. There were rare species blooming that they knew only from books. Park rangers declared it the "Hundred-Year Bloom," something that no one living had ever seen.

Badwater Basin, normally so harsh and desolate, became an ephemeral lake, deep enough for kayakers to say that they had kayaked Death Valley. Although shallow, it was large enough to be photographed by a NASA satellite. Badwater Lake evaporated in its entirety soon after.

These are some of the photographs of Mark Grieco as we undertook our own Death Valley trip that magnificent spring.

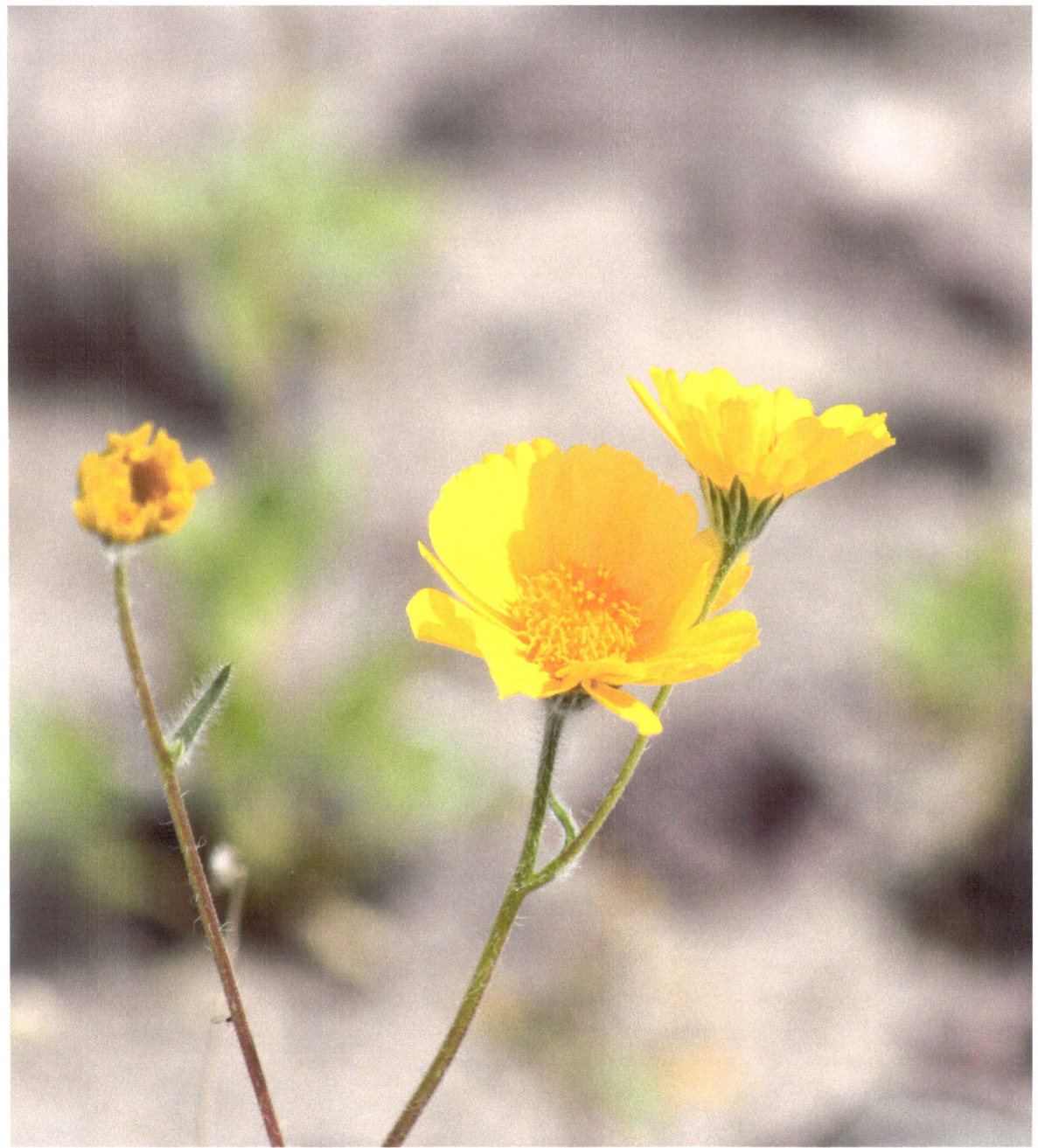

DESERT GOLD
By far the most prolific wildflower in Death Valley that spring,
desert gold could be found in nearly every region of the park.

(opposite page)

Even with an abundance of wildflowers, the rocky and
normally barren soil of Death Valley is plainly visible.

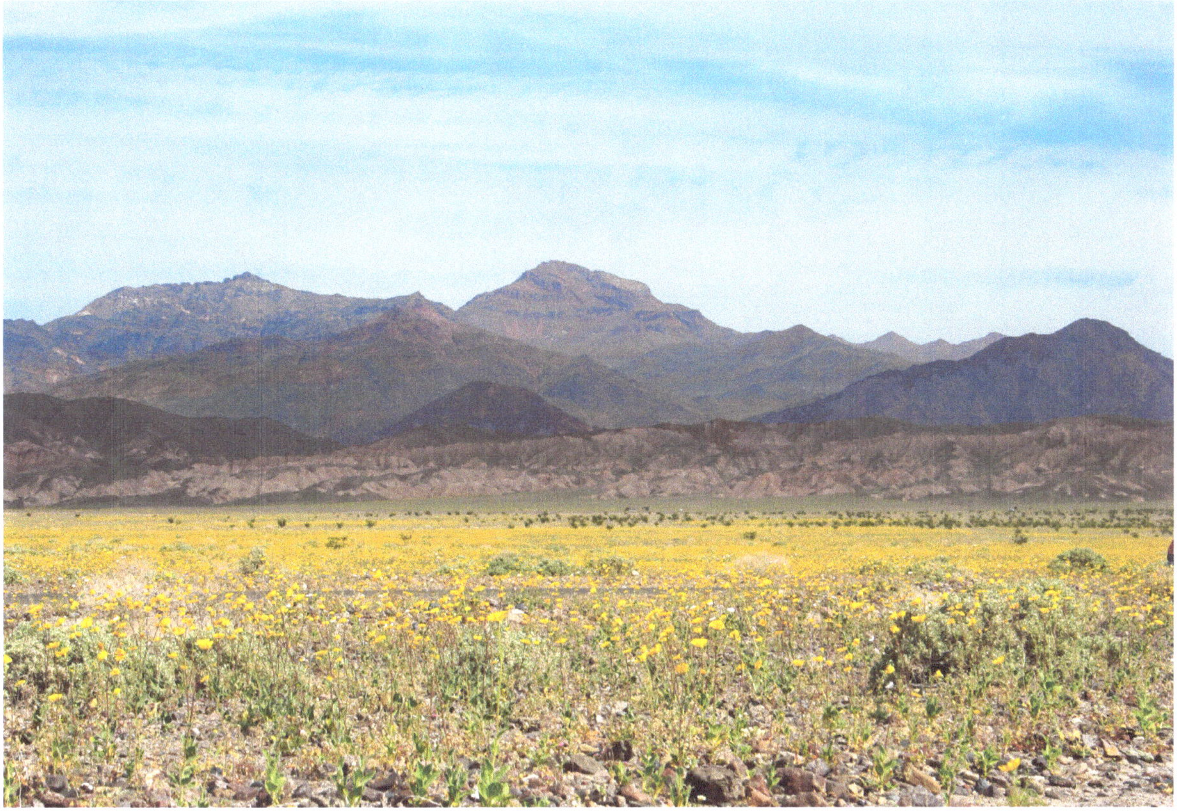

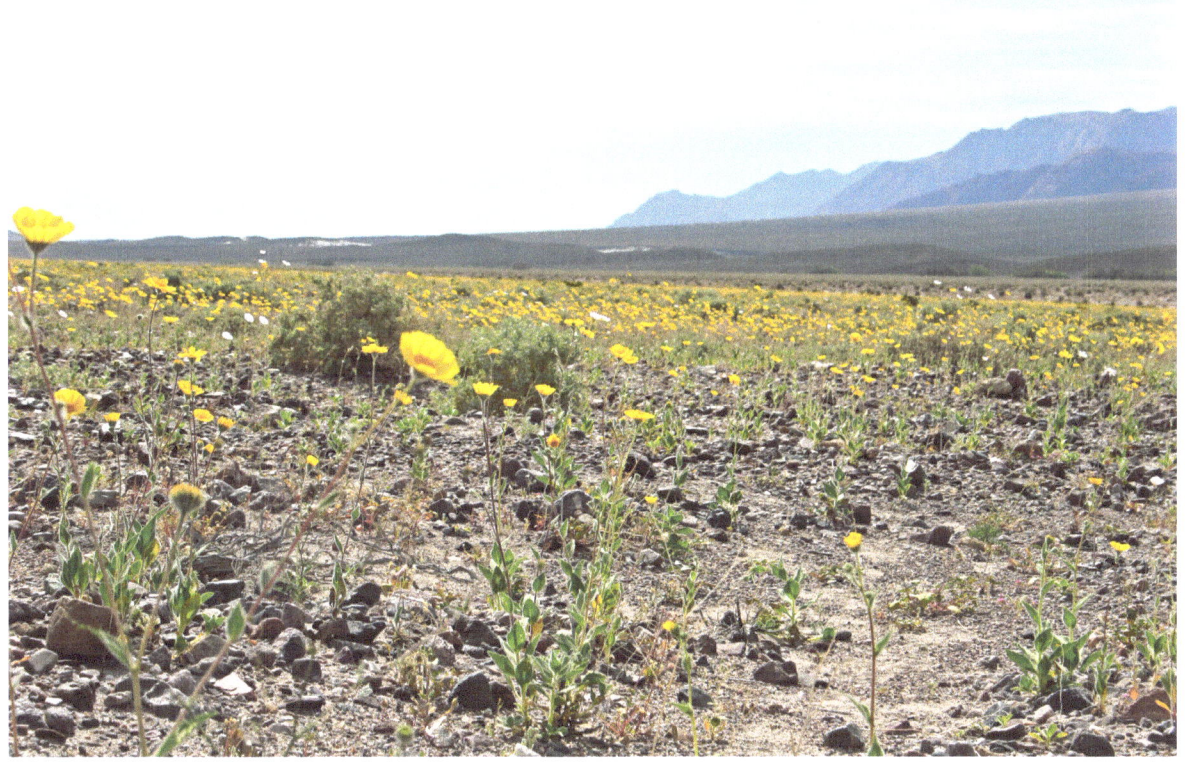

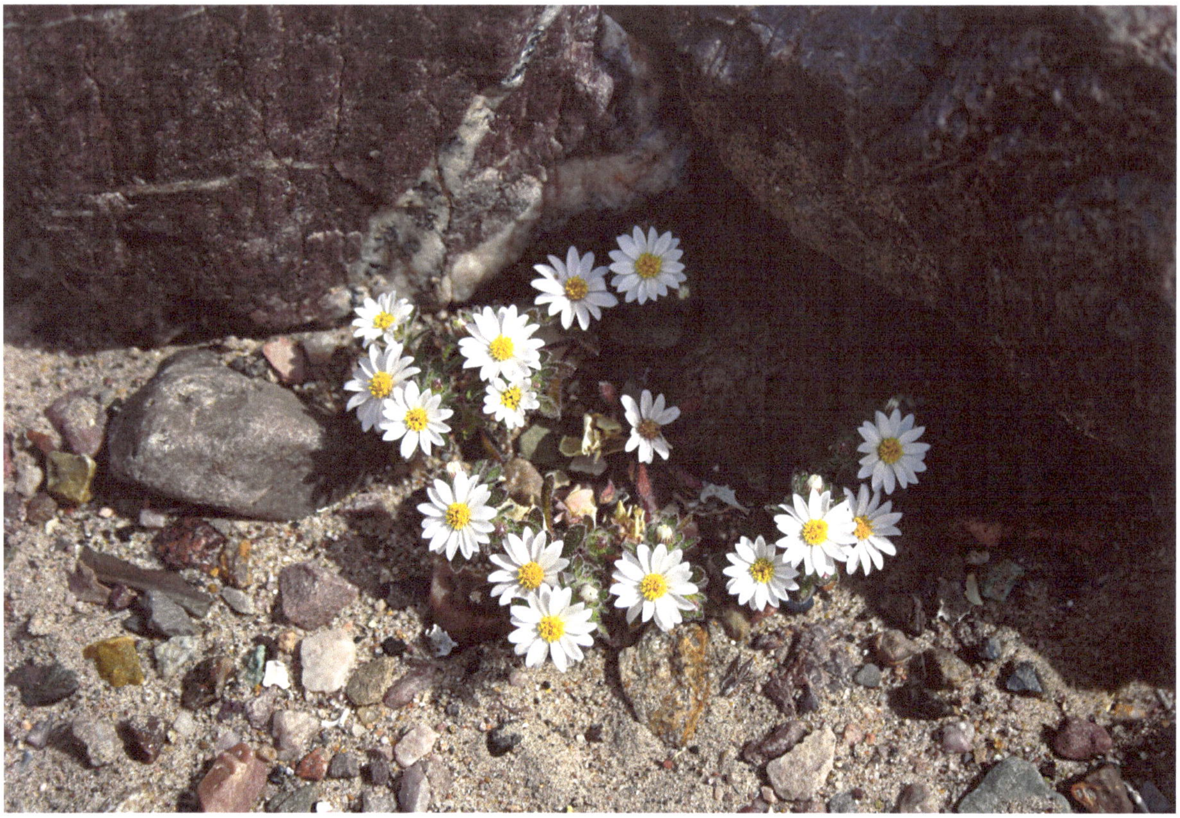

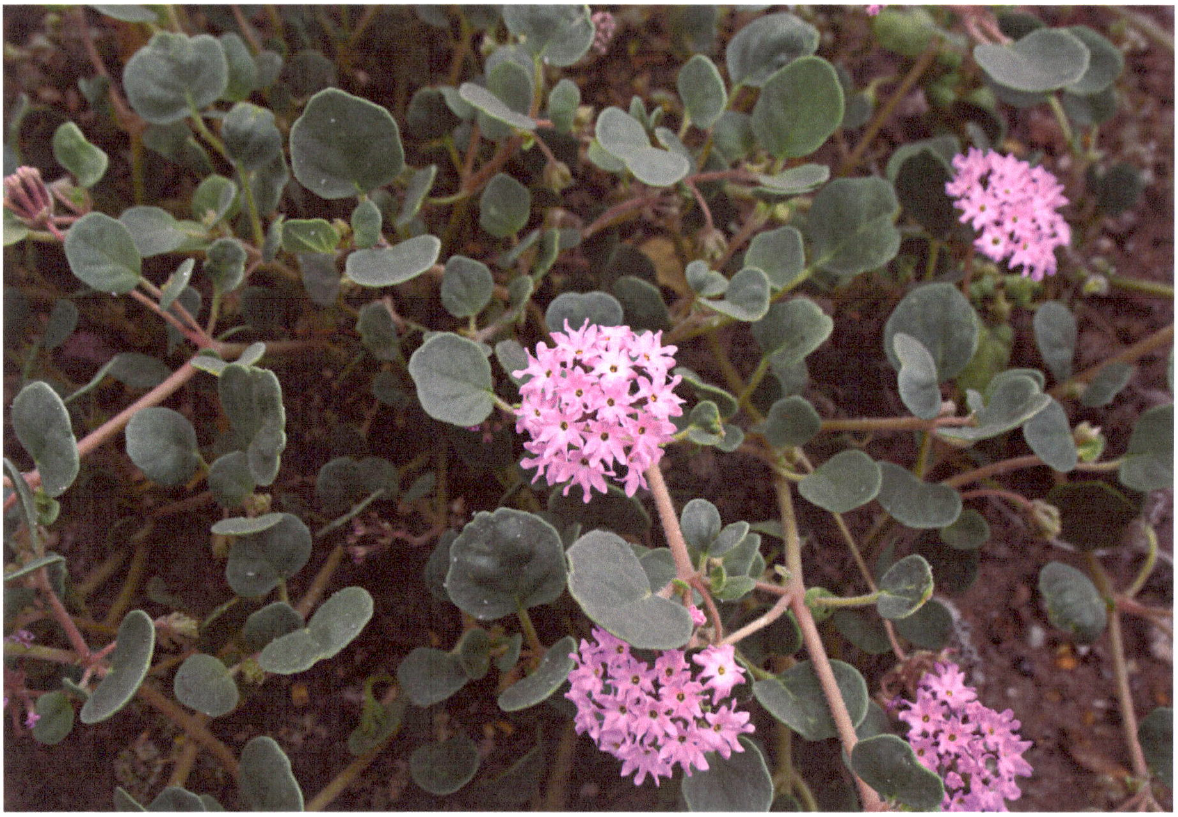

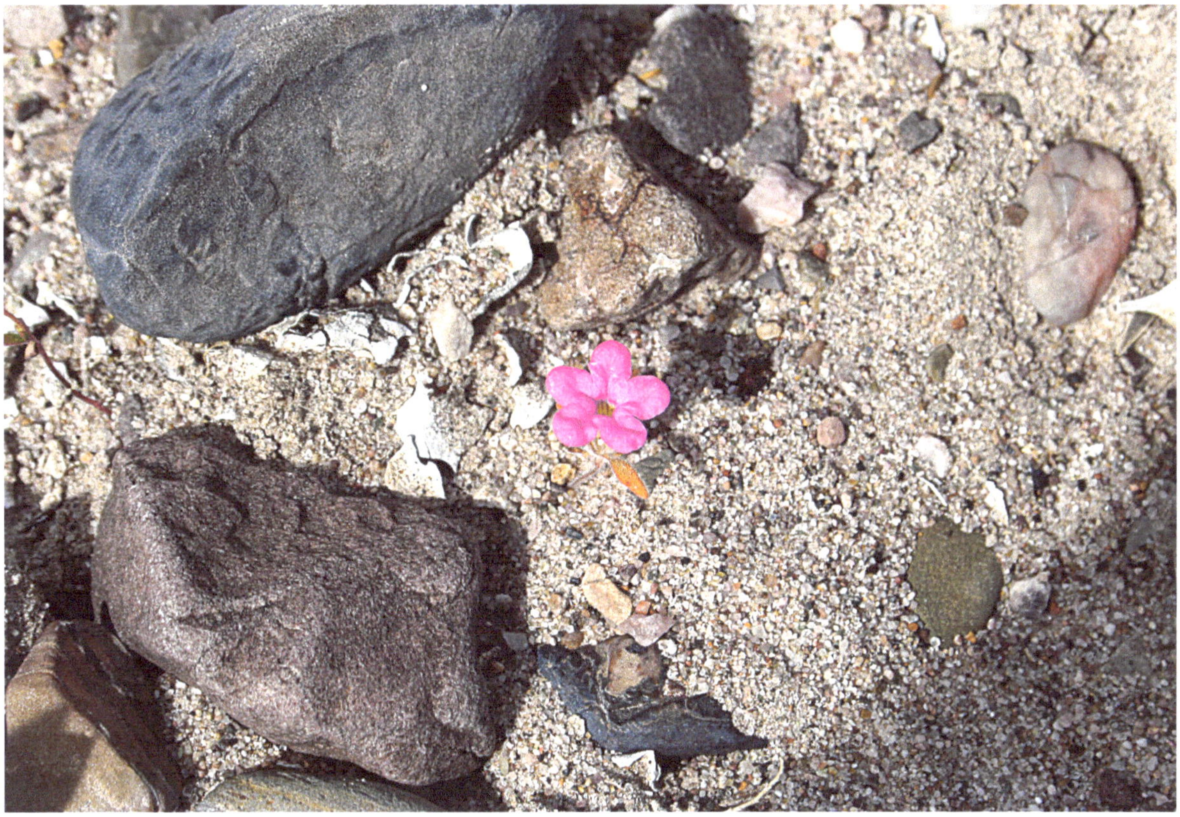

PURPLE MAT
(*top*)
Normally purple mat blooms in clusters.
Here a seed put all of its energy into a
single, tiny blossom.

BOOTH'S EVENING PRIMROSE
(*bottom*)

(*opposite page*)

DESERT STAR
(*top*)
A minute flower, about a thumbnail's
width across.

SAND VERBENA
(*bottom*)

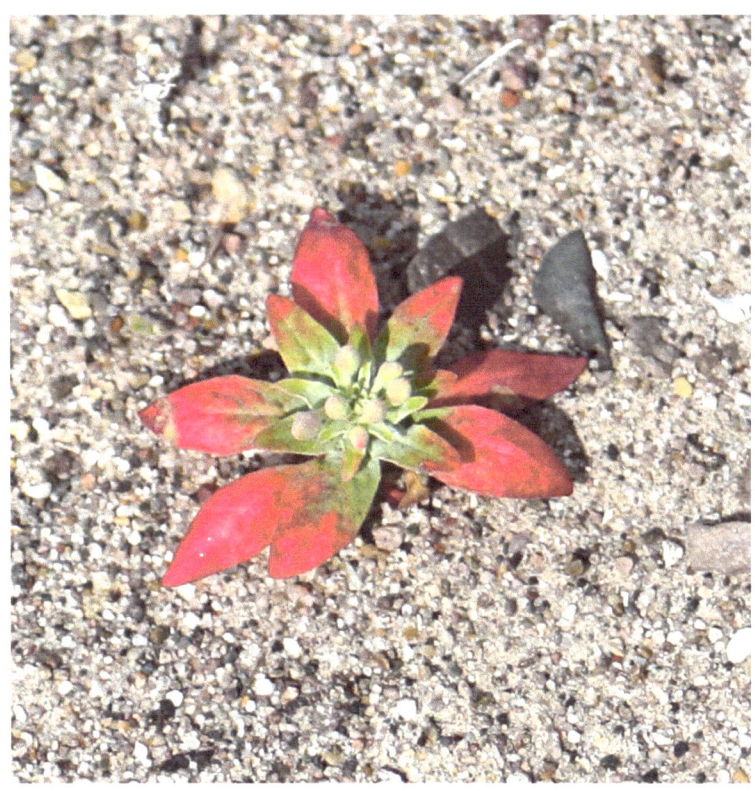

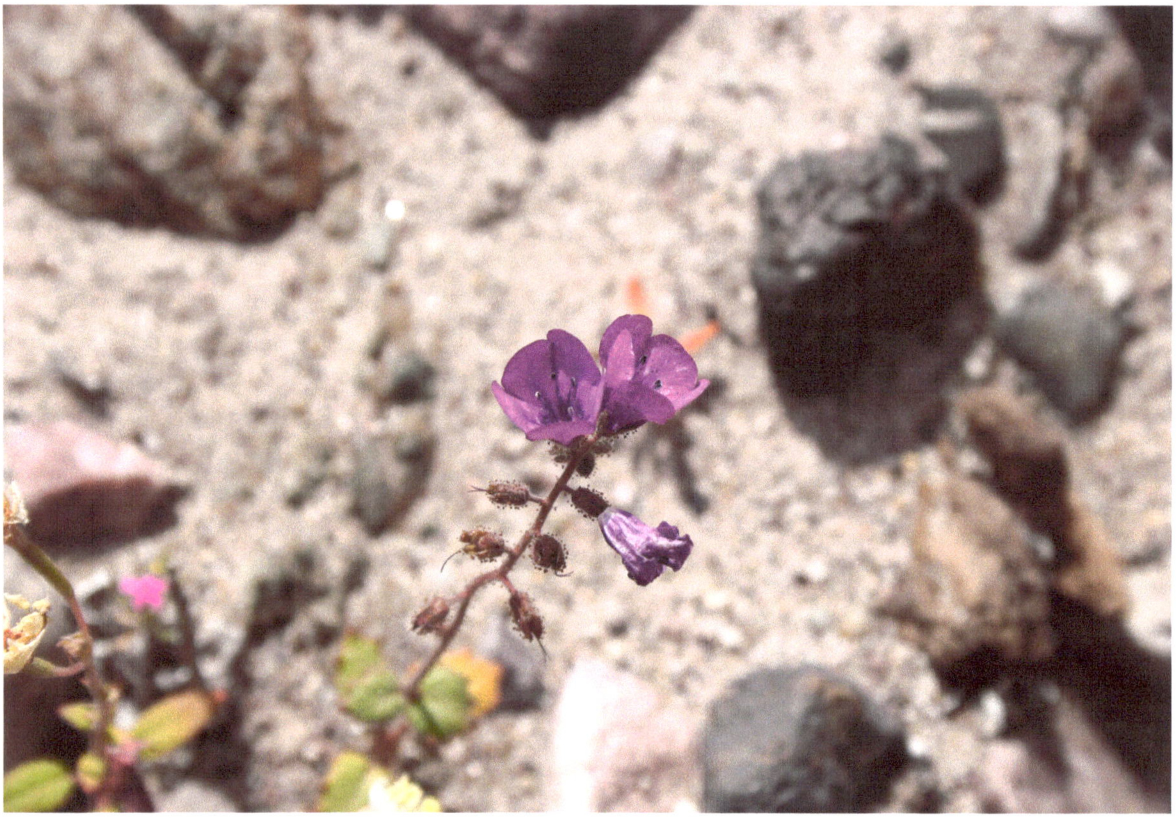

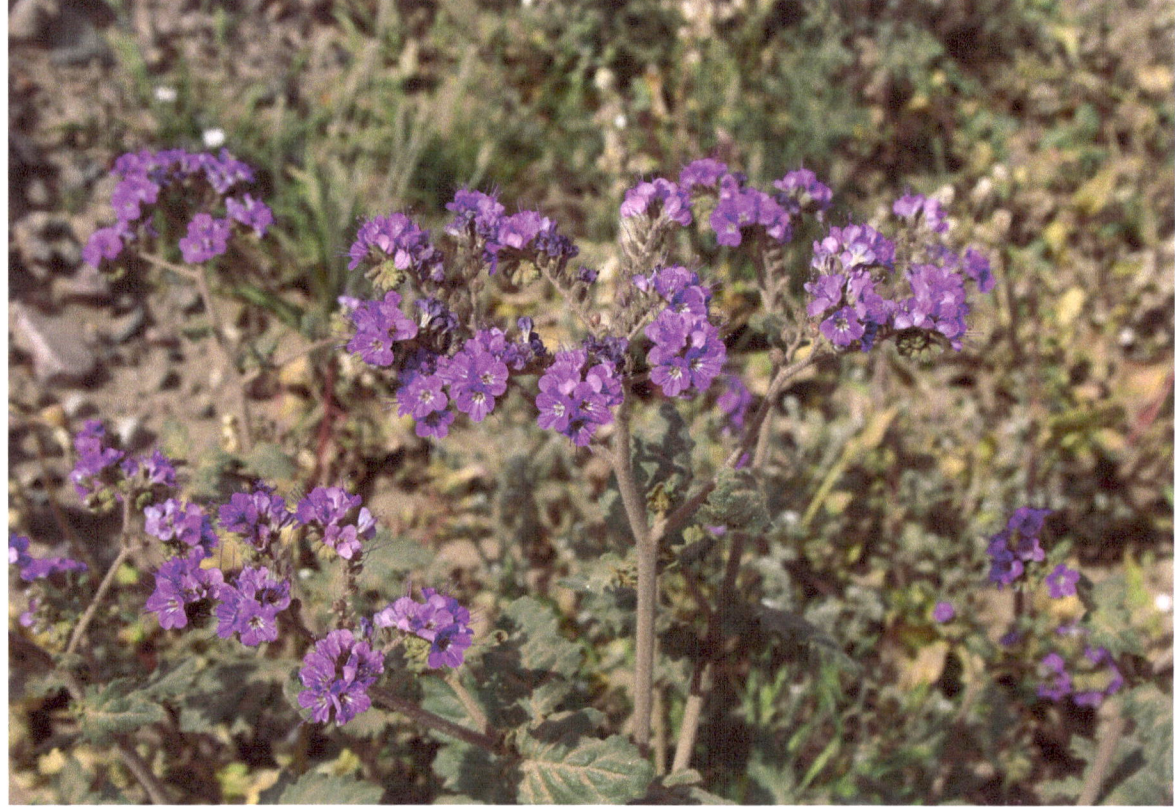

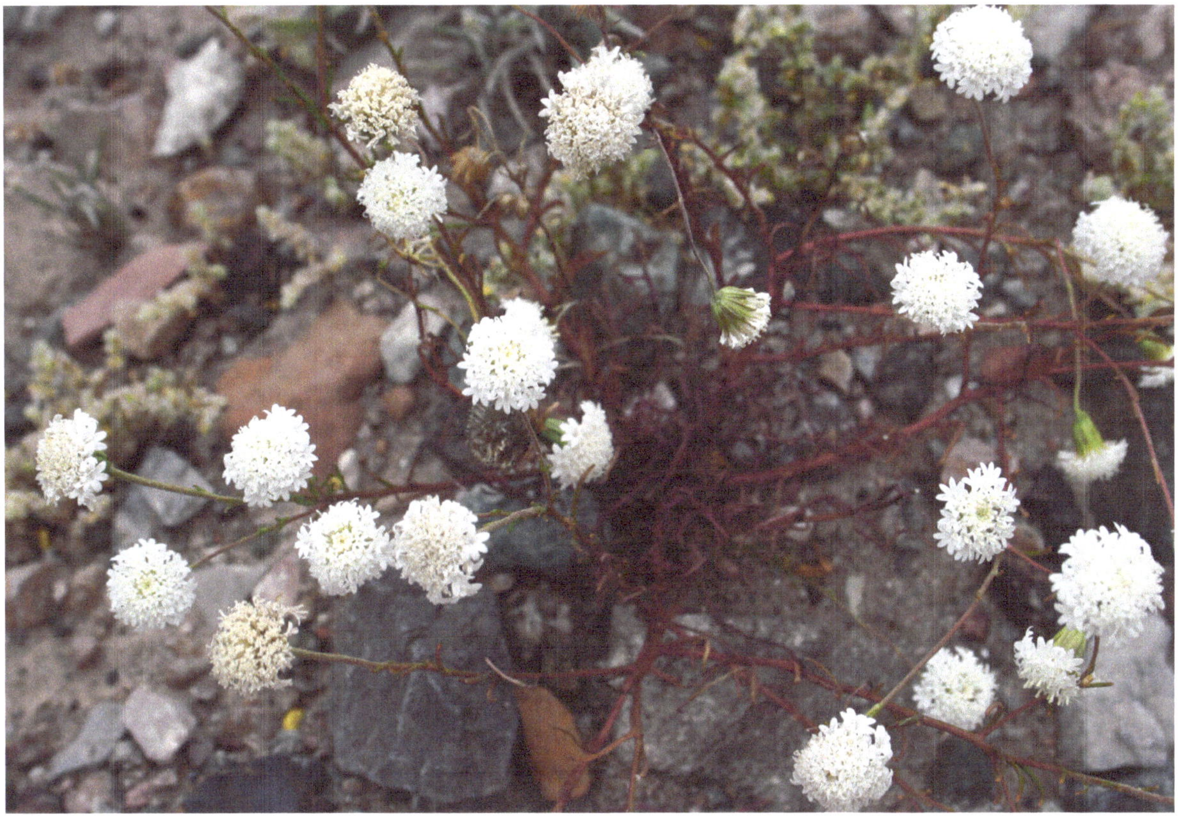

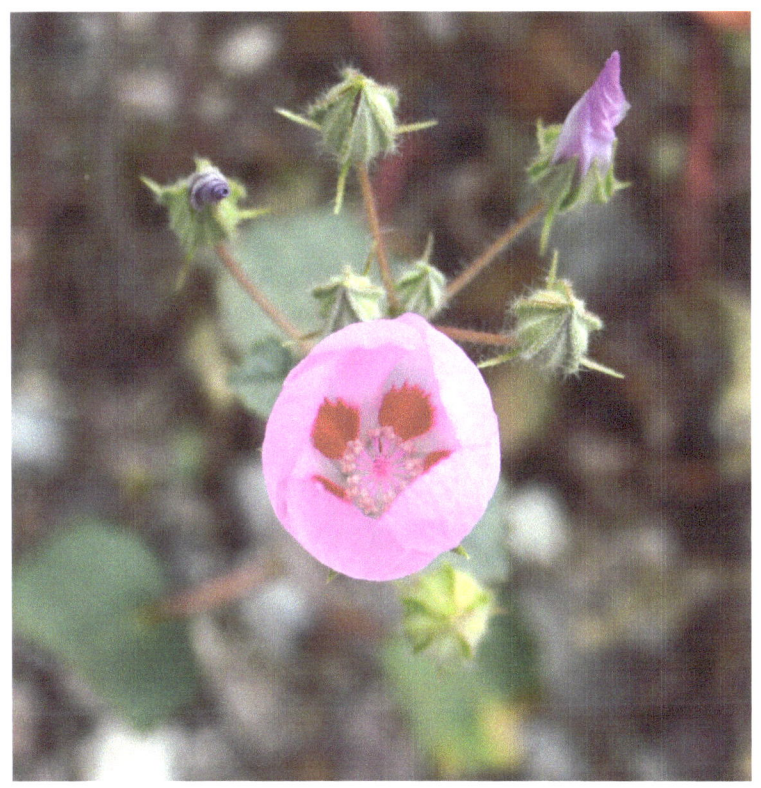

FREMONT PINCUSHION
(top)

DESERT FIVE-SPOT
(bottom)

(opposite page)

CALTHALEAF PHACELIA
(top)

NOTCHLEAF PHACELIA
(bottom)

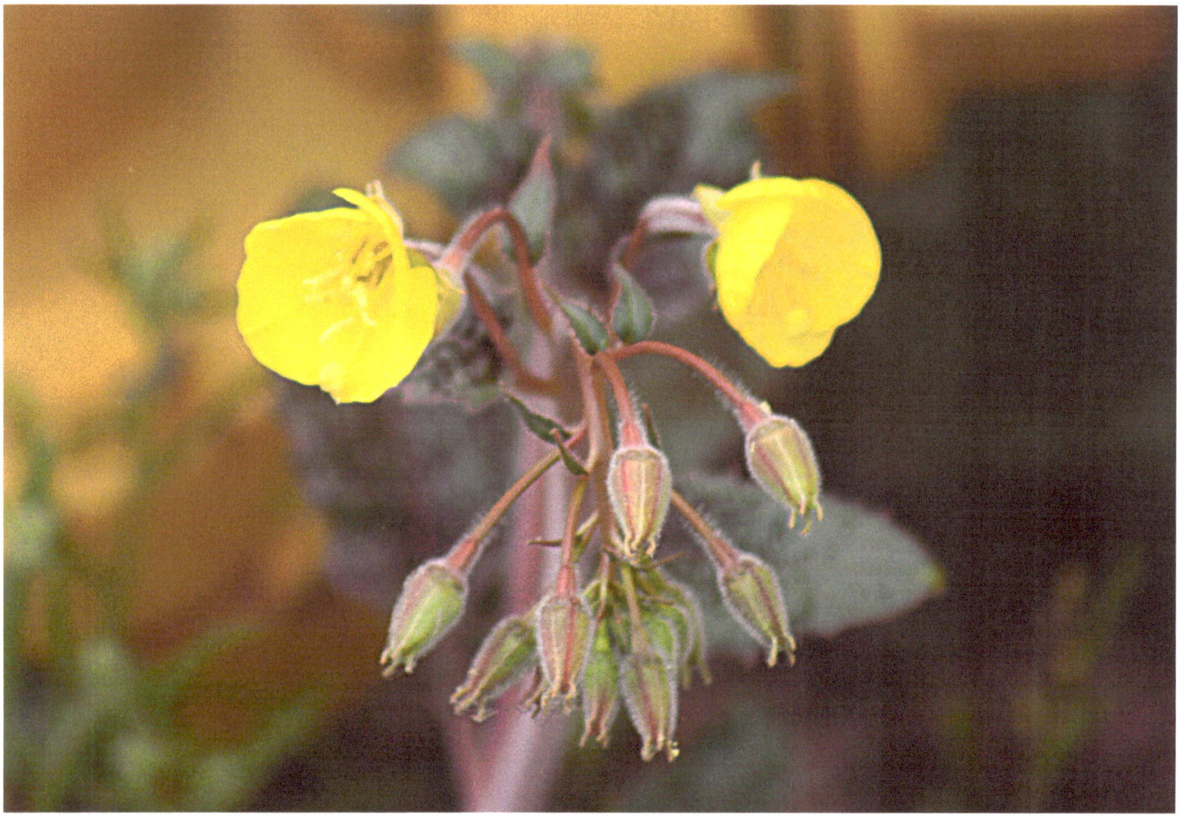

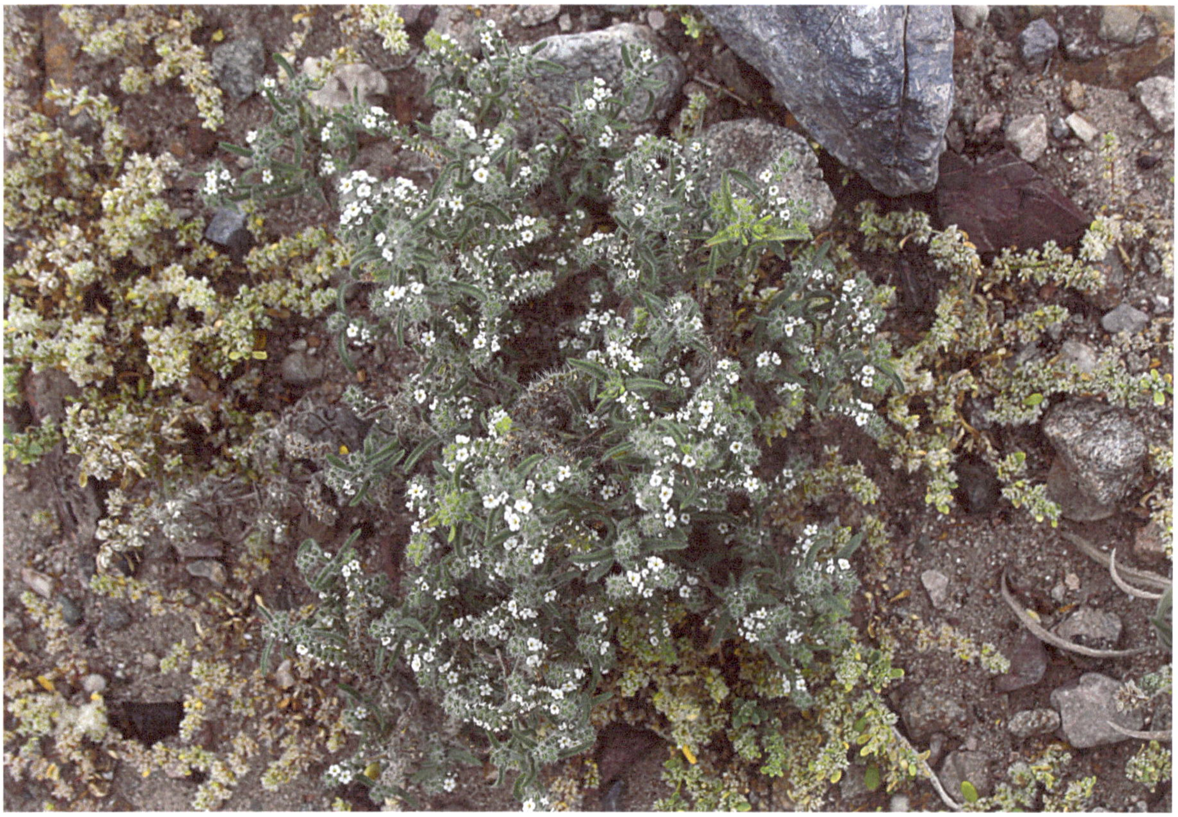

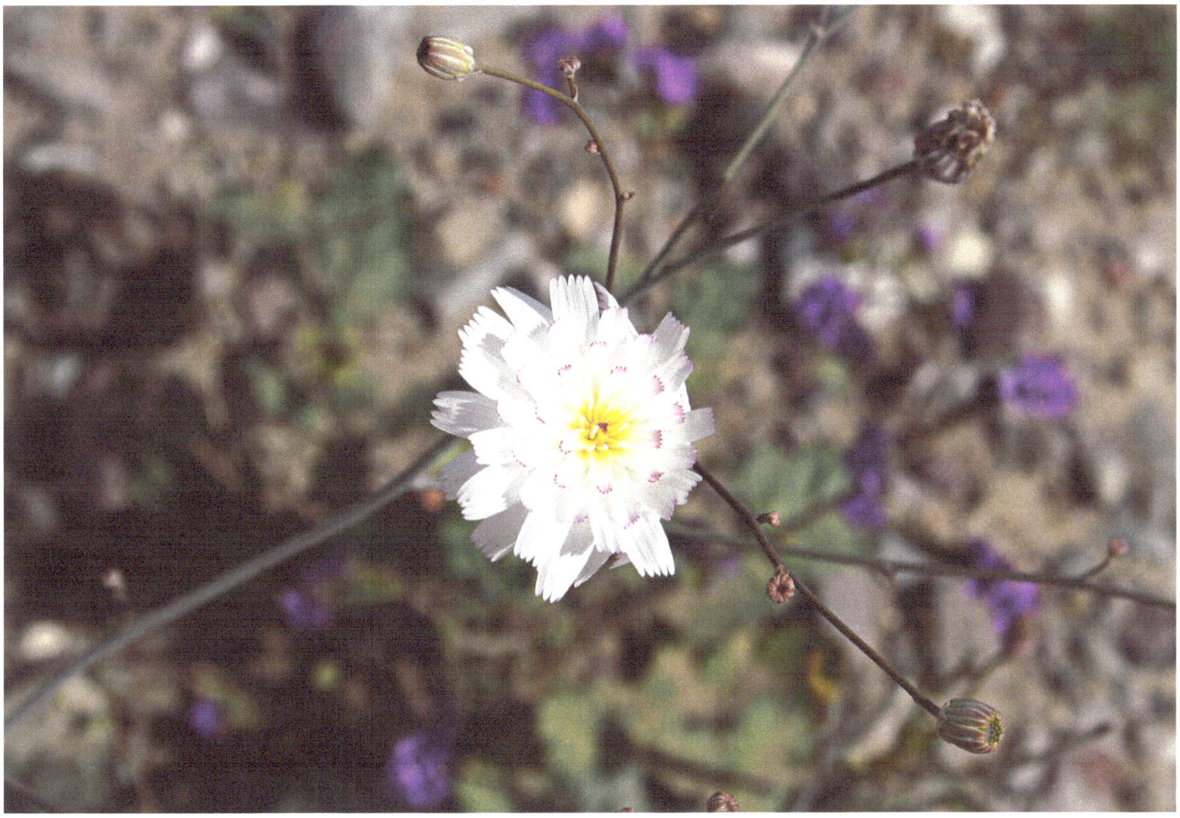

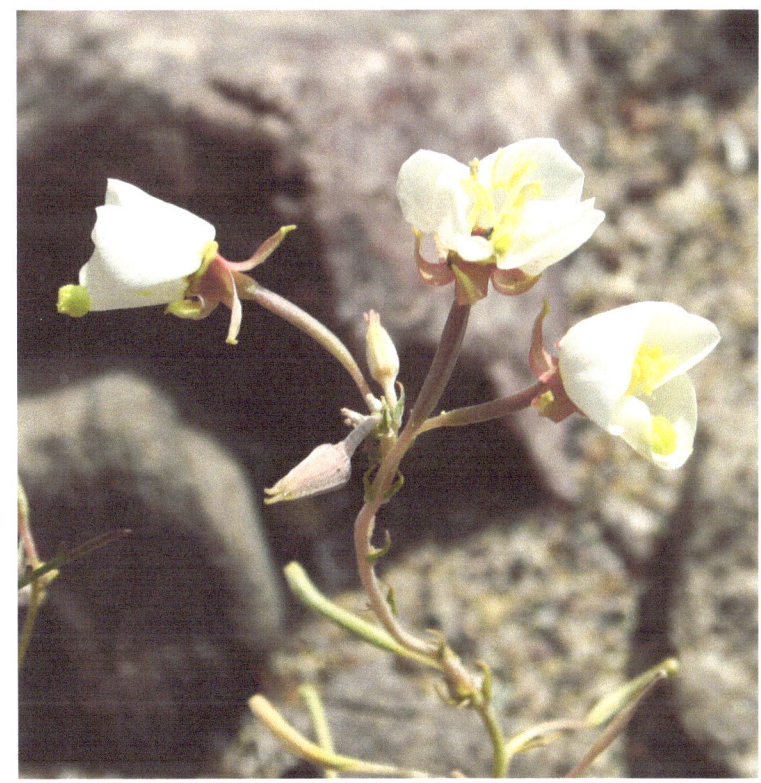

GRAVEL GHOST
(top)

BROWN-EYED PRIMROSE
(bottom)

(opposite page)

GOLDEN EVENING PRIMROSE
(top)

PANAMINT CRYPTANTHA
(bottom)

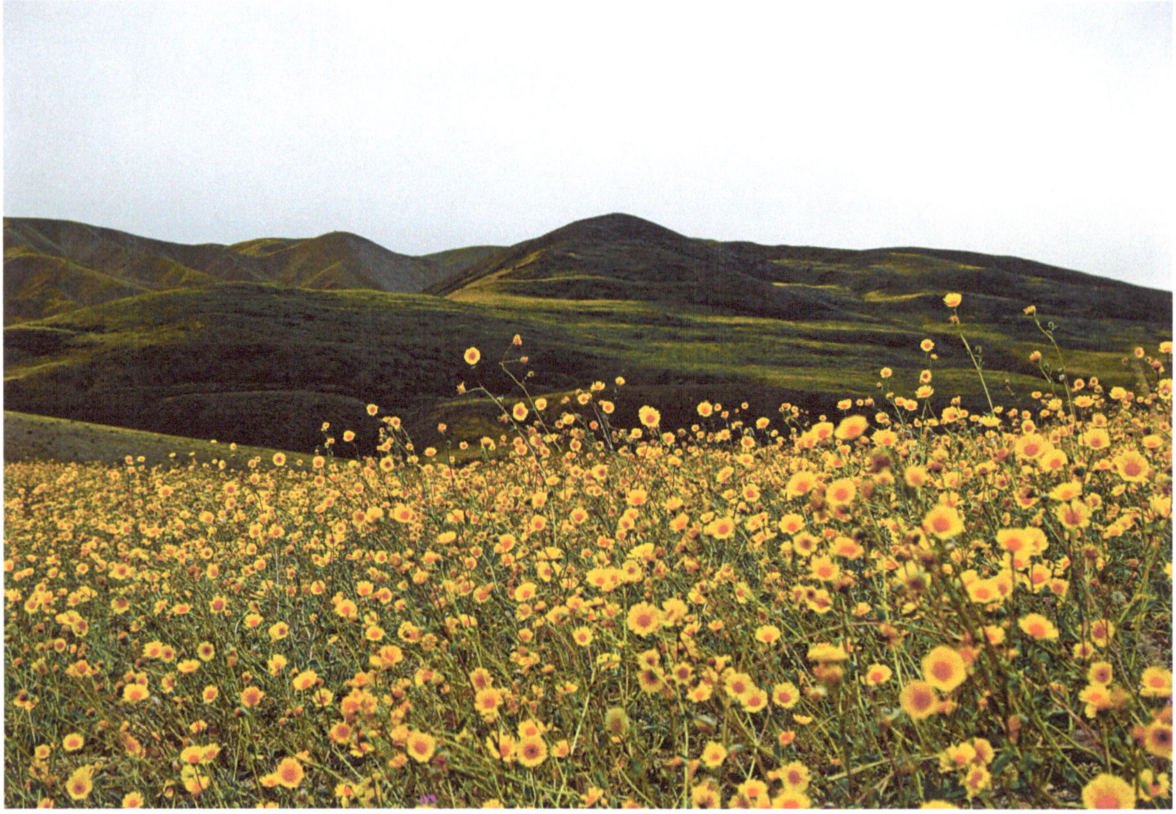

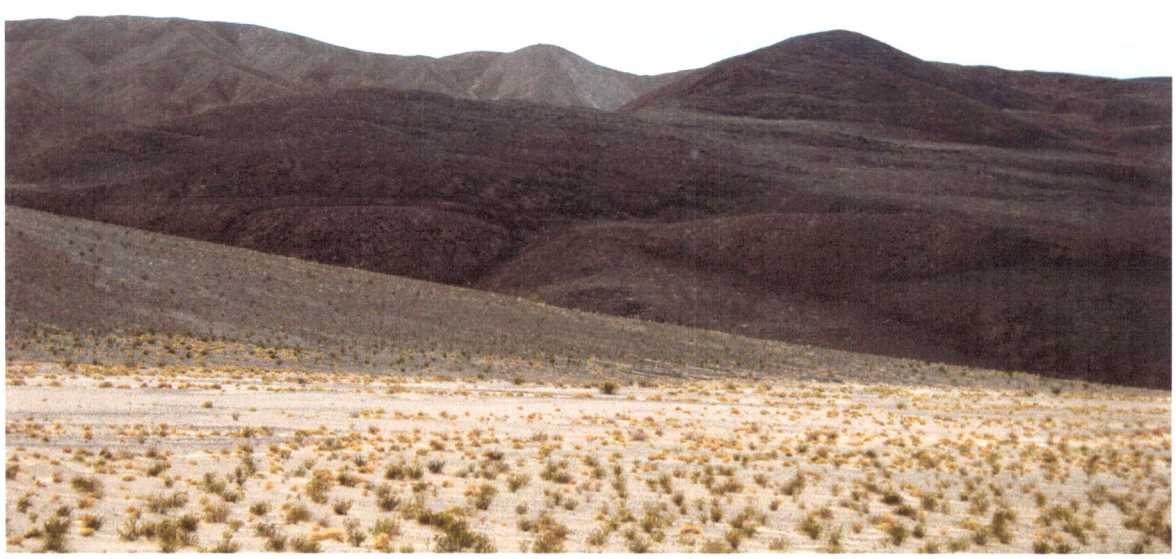

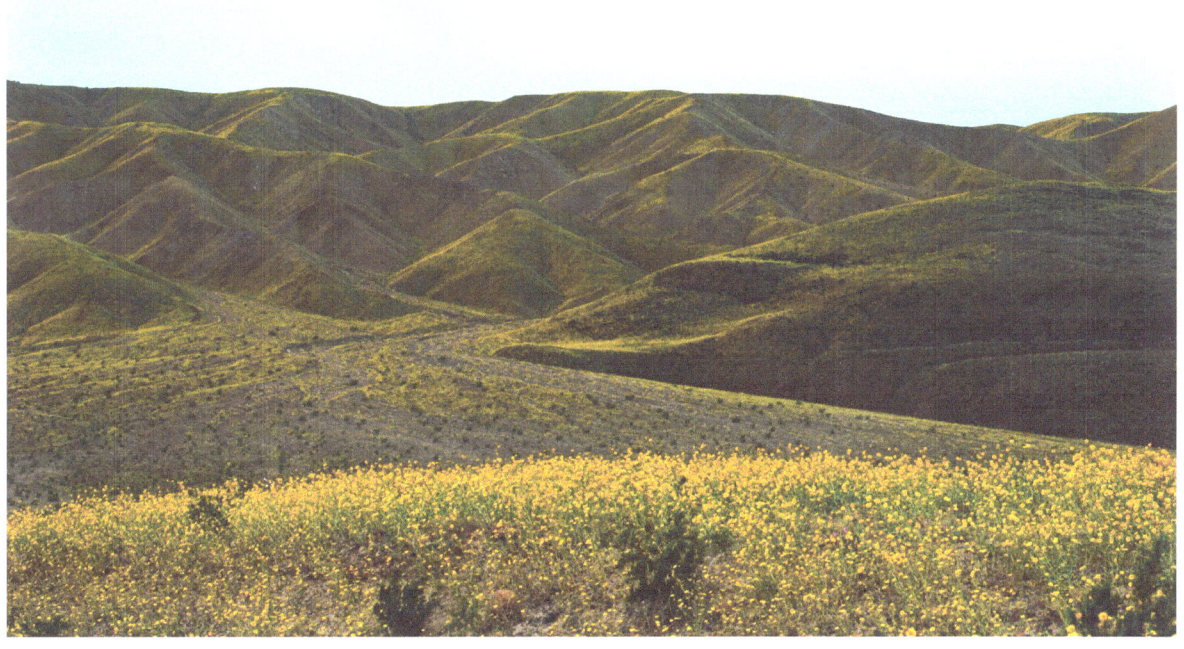

THE MIRACLE OF RAIN
One reason the Hundred-Year Bloom
was so astonishing can be seen in
the dramatic transformation of the
landscape.

(opposite page)

ASHFORD MILL
(top)
The carpet of wildflowers at Ashford
Mill in the spring of 2005.

(bottom)
Ashford Mill, seen with more typical
vegetation.

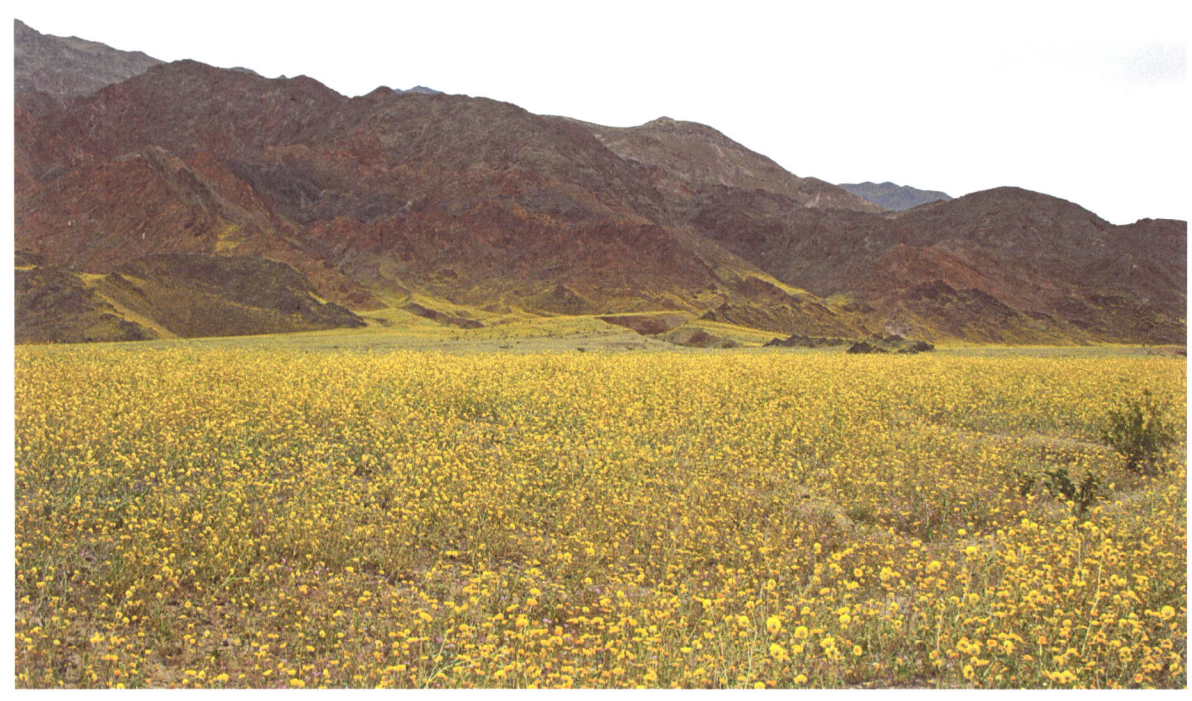

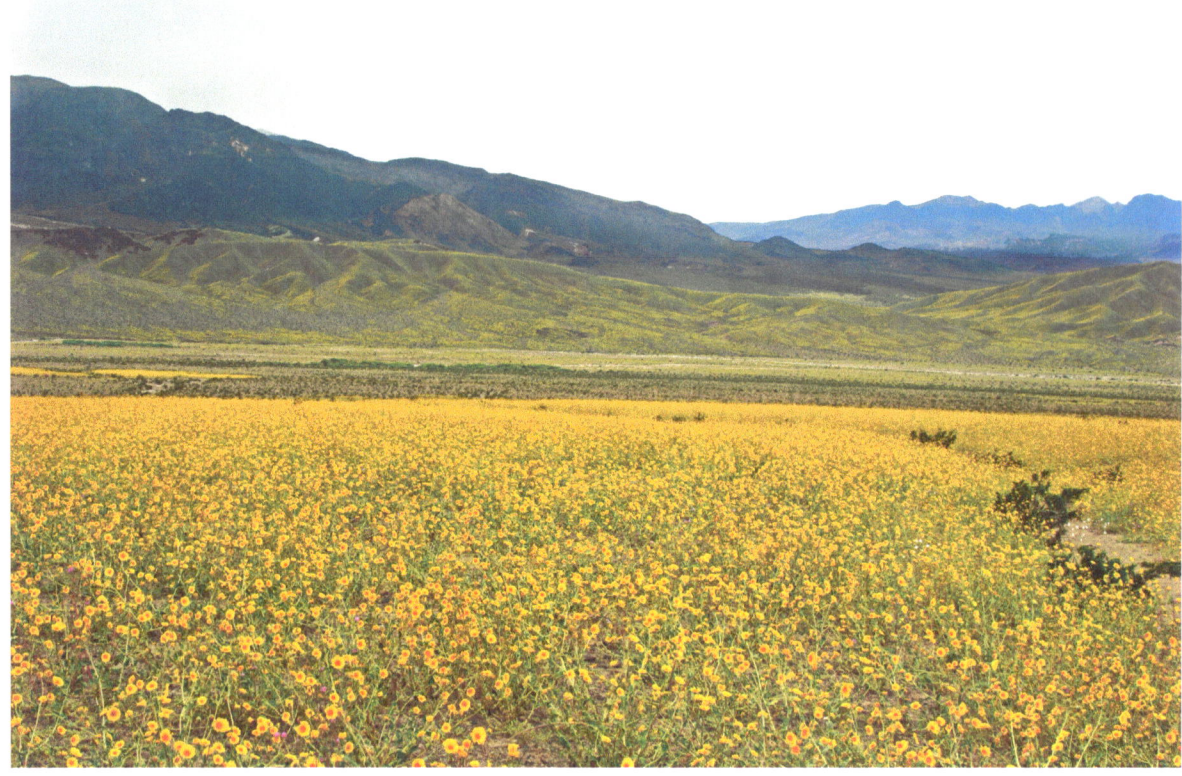

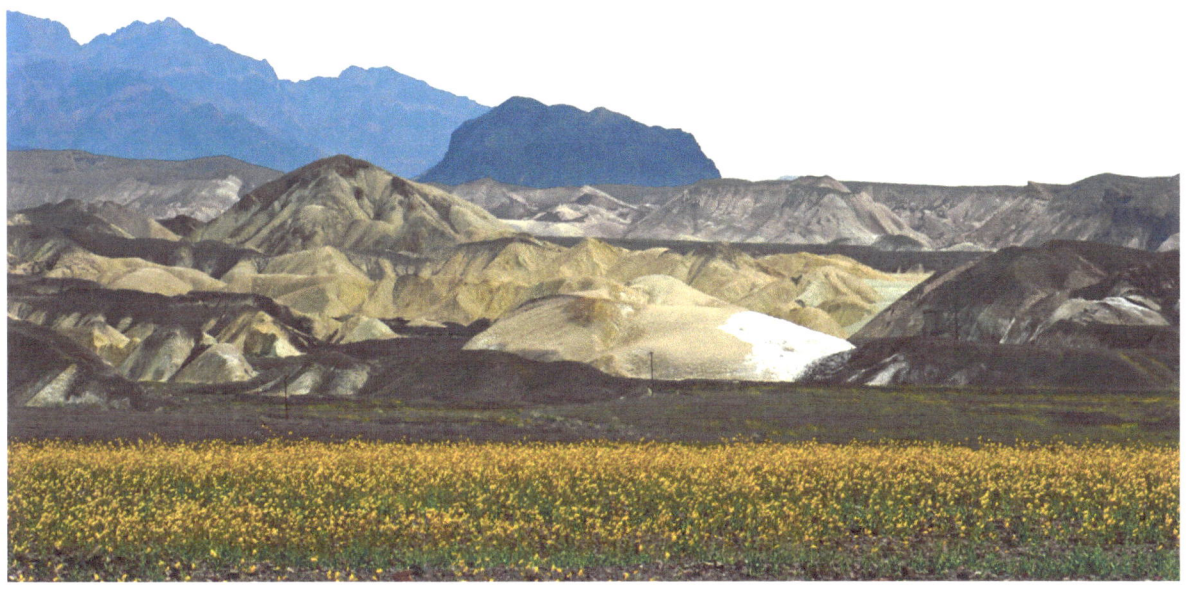

RICH PALETTE
Death Valley's geological history can be
seen in the myriad colors of its hills and
mountains.

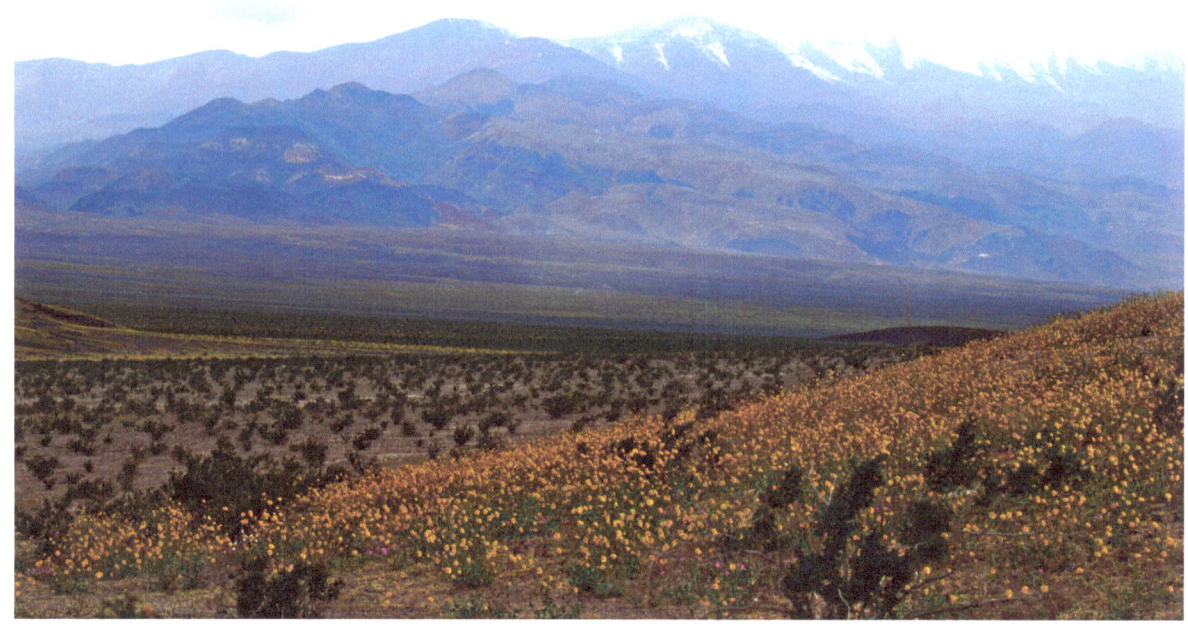

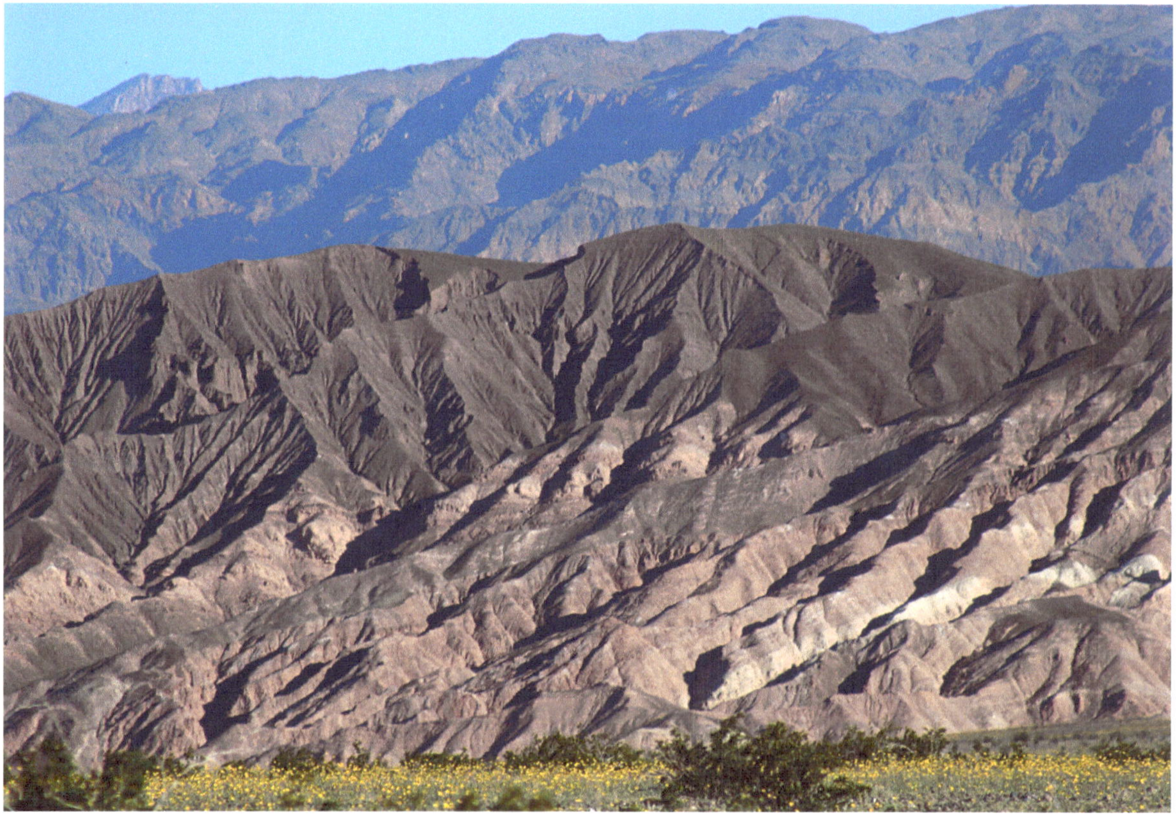

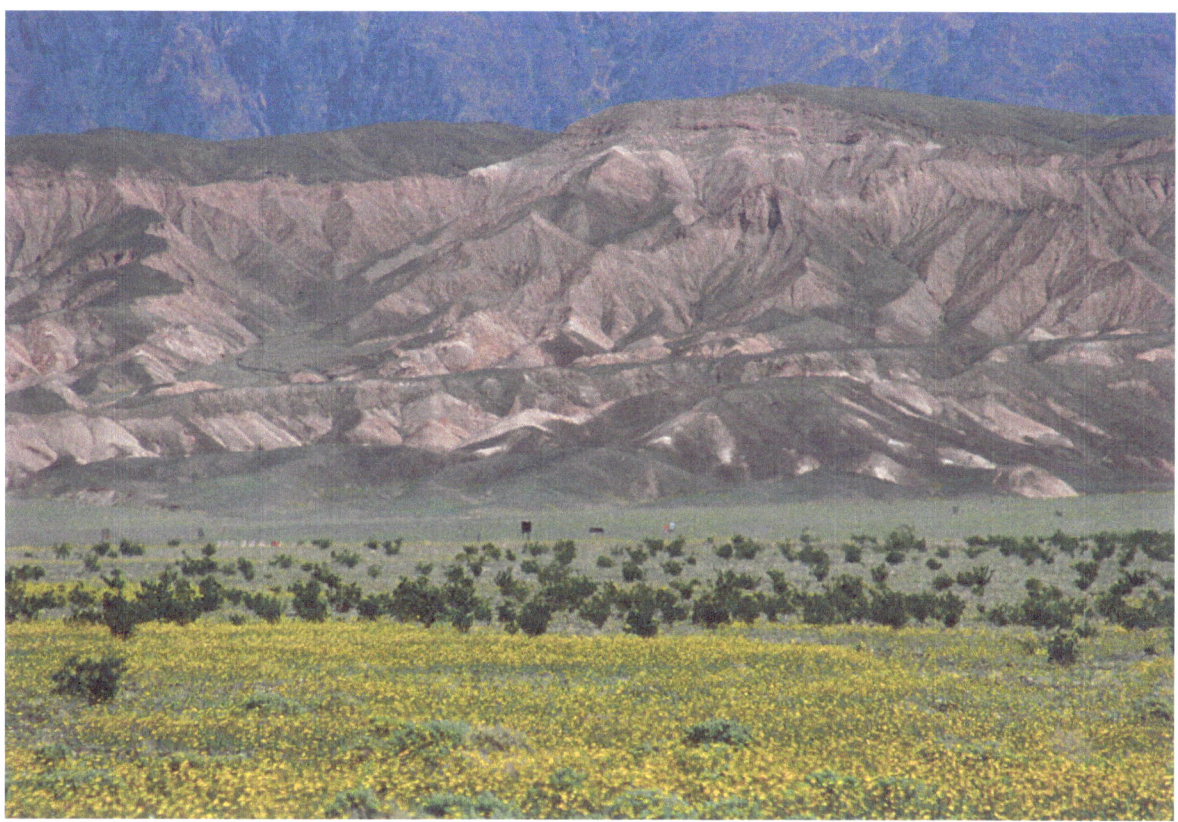

MOUNTAIN VISTAS

At almost every point in Death Valley
is a stunning view of its surrounding
mountains—the Grapevine, Owlshead,
Black, Funeral and Cottonwood
mountains, among others.

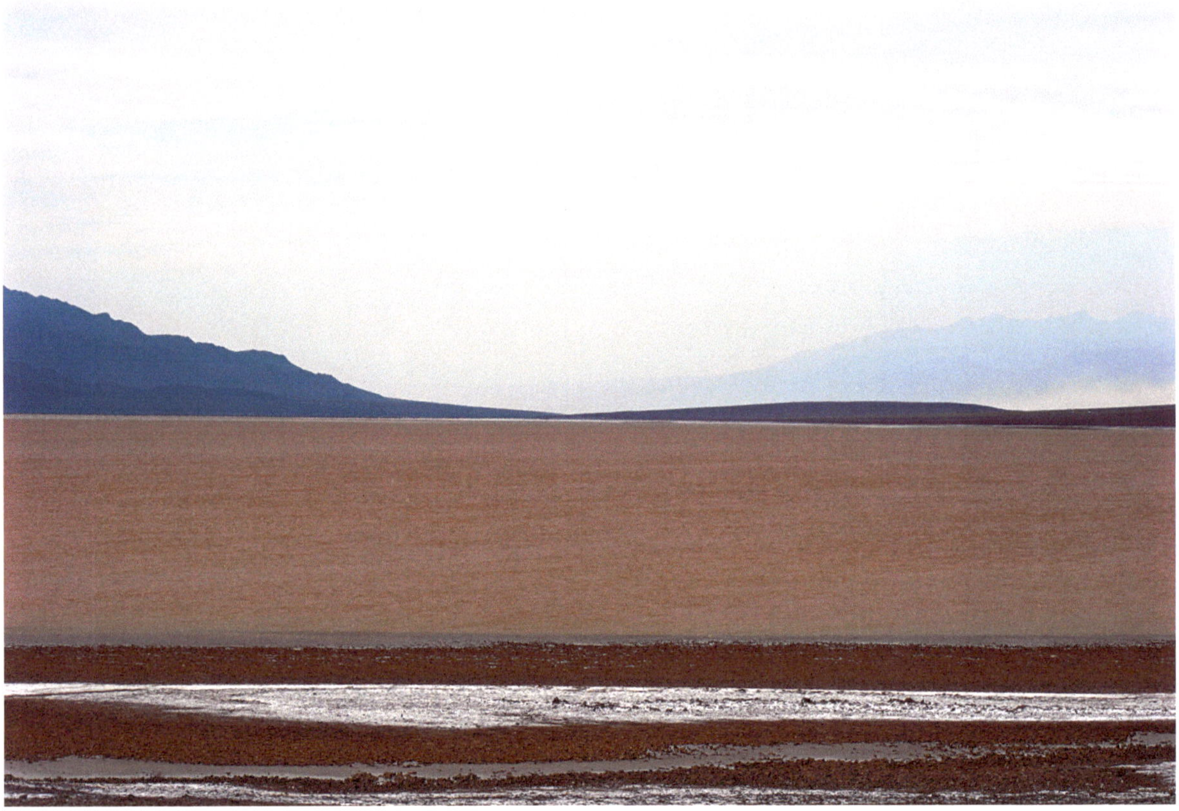

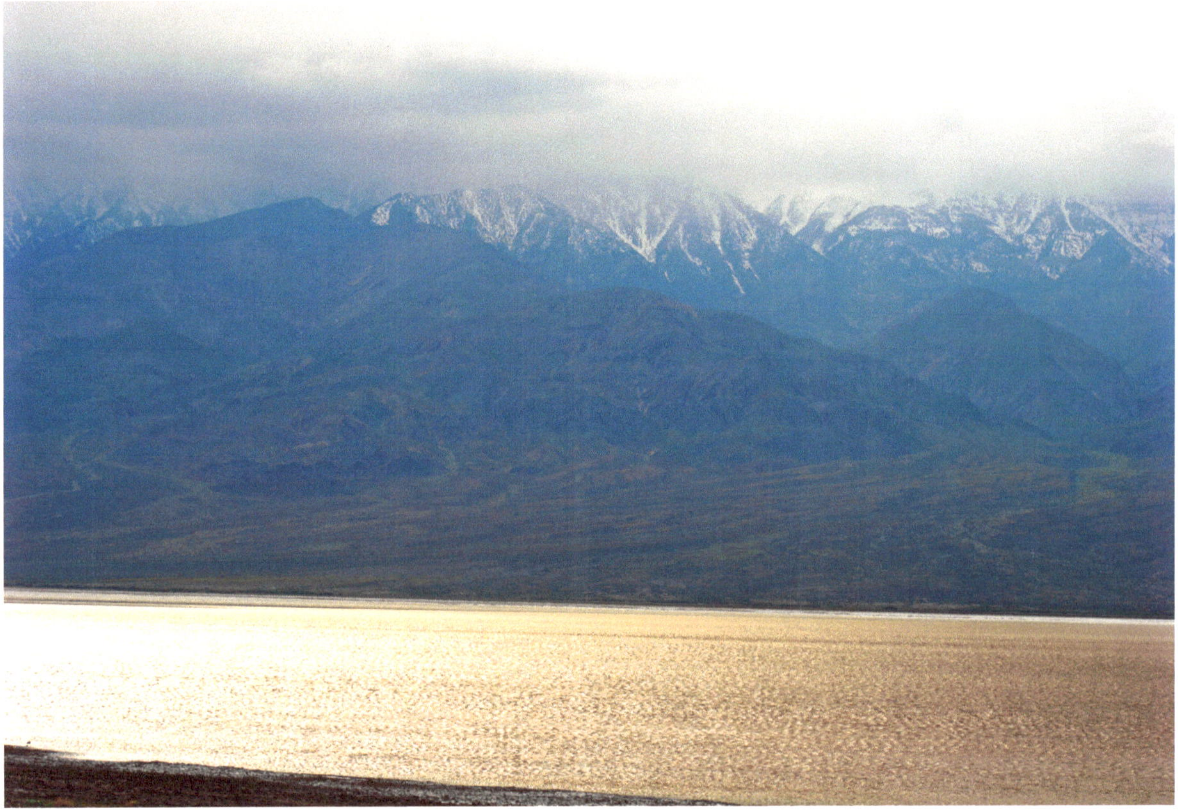

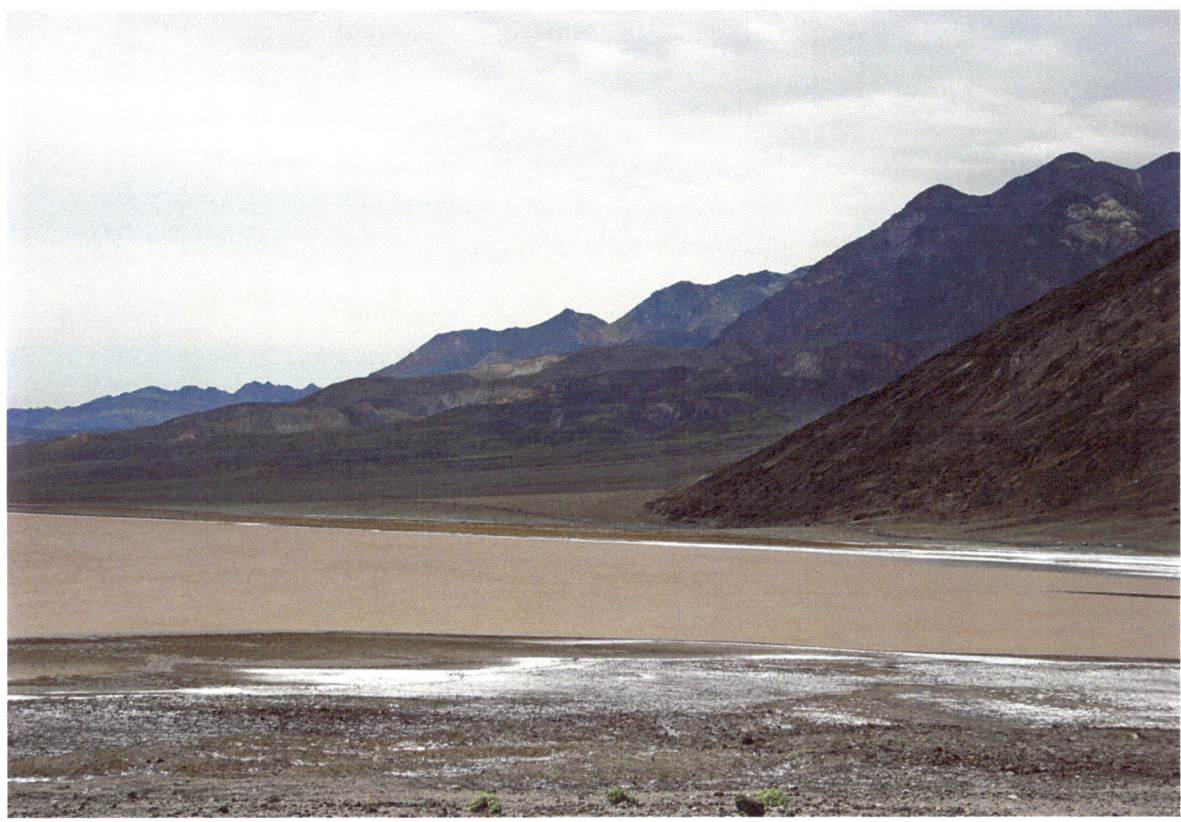

BADWATER "LAKE"

So much rain fell in the winter of
2004–05 that Badwater Basin became
an ephemeral lake, quite large but
very shallow. Because of the soil's high
salinity, the water was also quite buoyant.

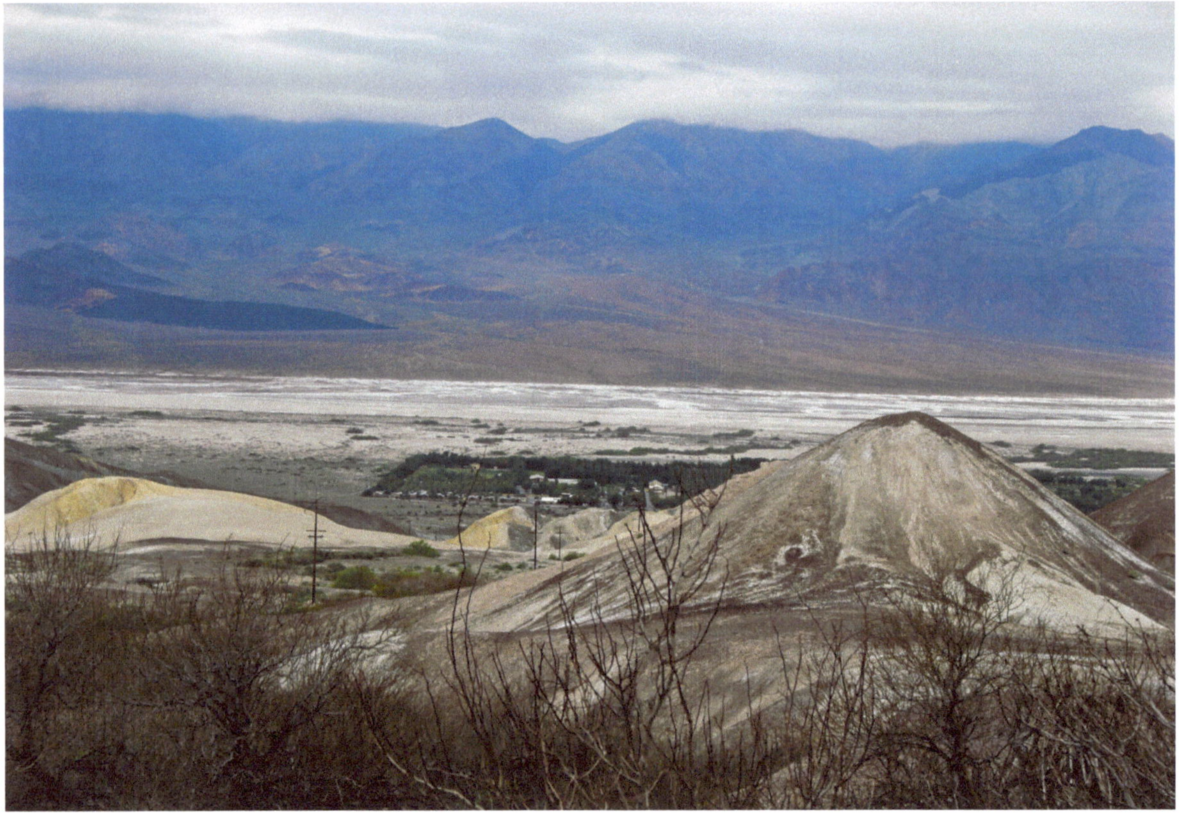

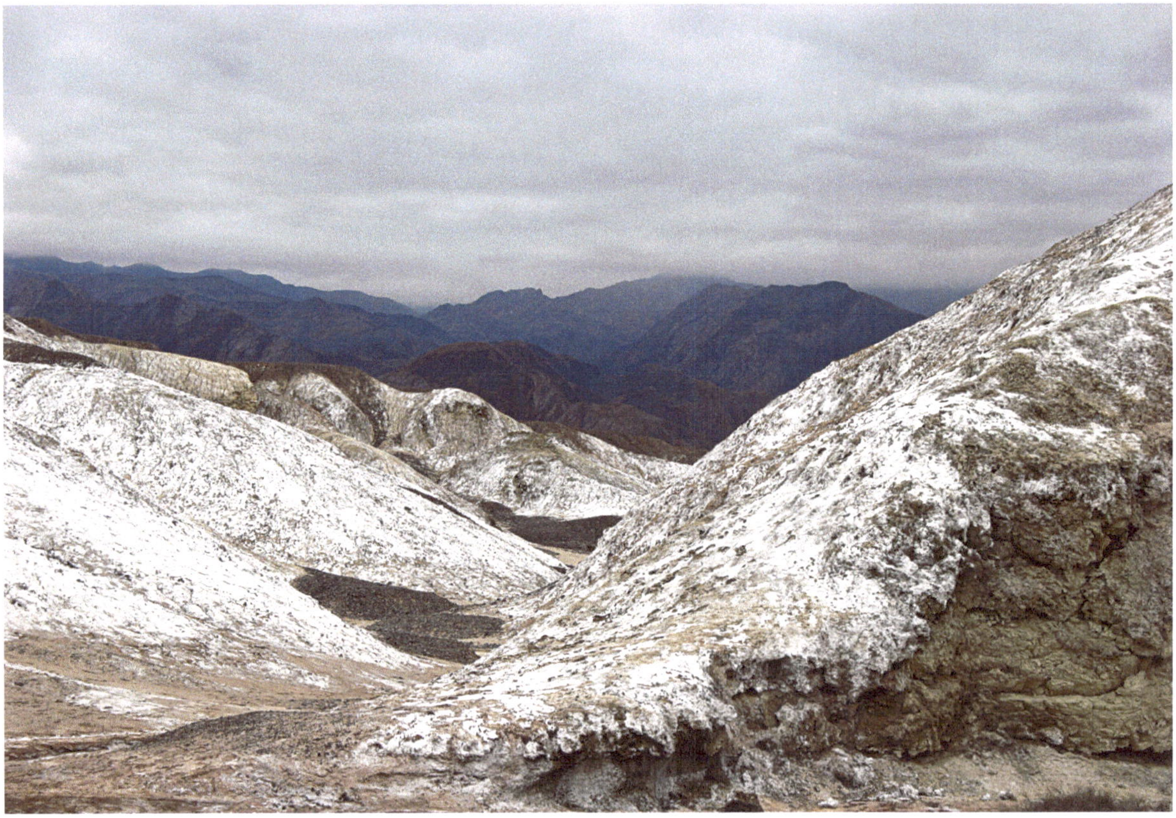

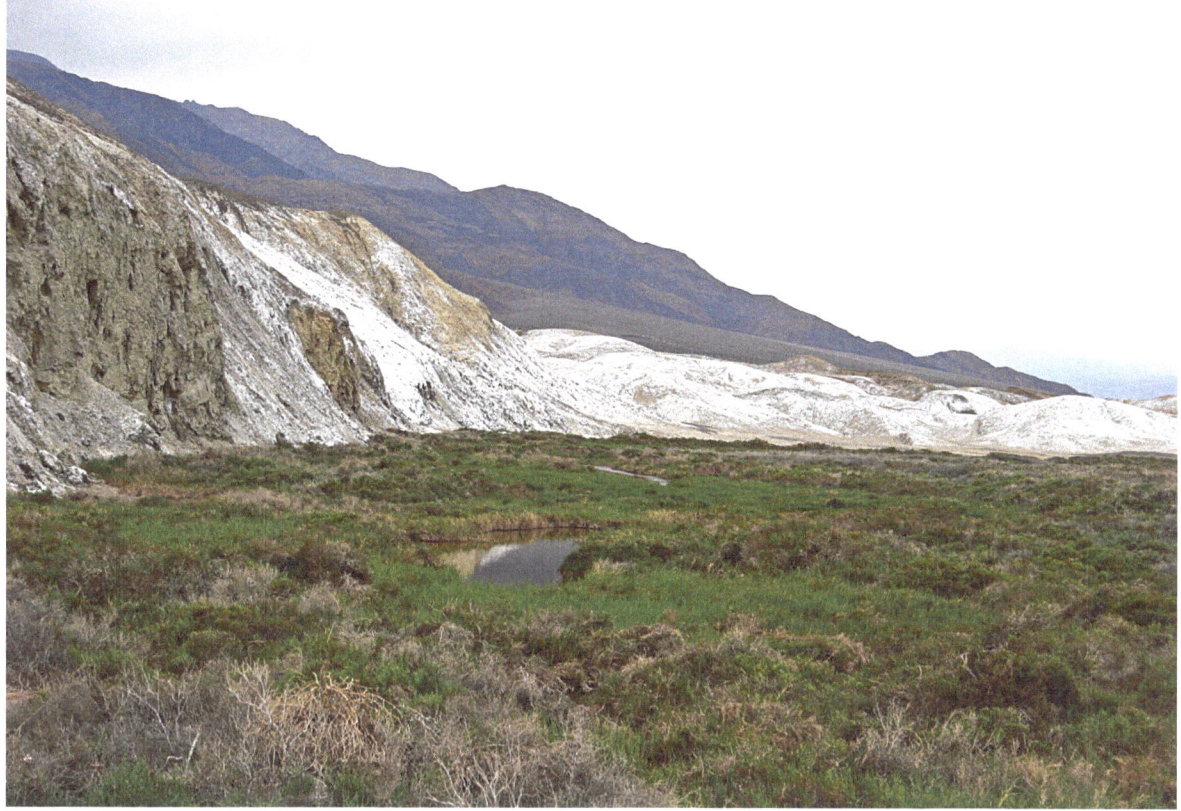

SALT CREEK
(top)
Salt Creek is home to the pupfish, which thrives in water reaching 90 degrees. Originally a species in the lakes that once covered Death Valley, they were trapped in small bodies of water when the lakes receded. Over time they adapted to the warm and increasingly briny water. The Devil's Hole pupfish, confined to a small body of water in nearby Nevada, evolved into a separate species so rare the total number of fish can be counted in the low hundreds.

(opposite page)

MOONSCAPE
Salts and mineral deposits are plainly visible on the ground. Death Valley's evaporation rate is so rapid that whatever dissolved minerals that are in rain water or mountain runoff crystallize as they are left behind.

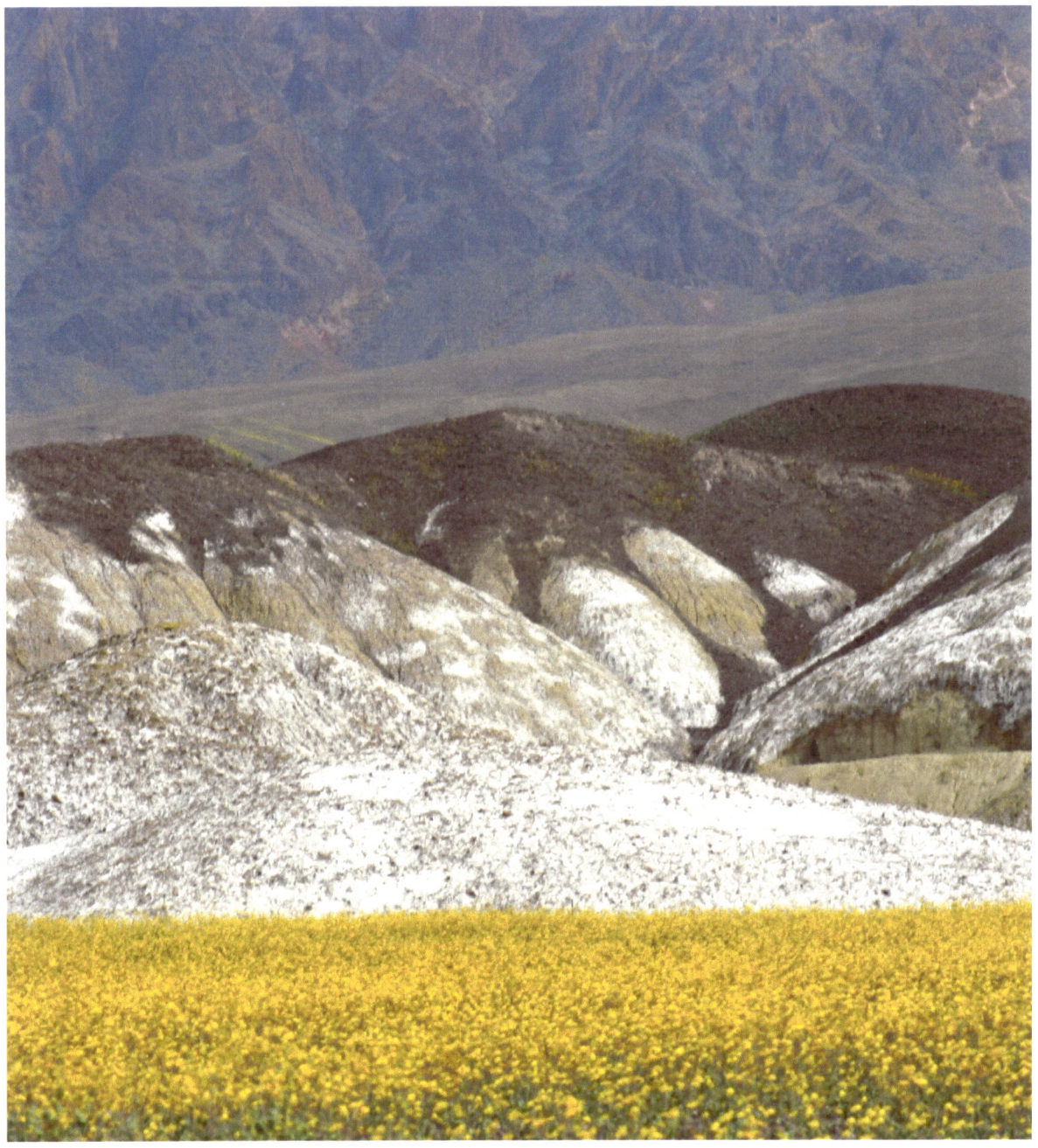

SUMMER SNOW
Like the pupfish, Death Valley's wildflowers
can tolerate the high-salt environment.

"Goodbye, Death Valley!"

The human history of Death Valley is a long one, going back as far as the end of the Ice Age, when the climate was more temperate and early inhabitants lived by marshes and streams. As the weather warmed and the water disappeared, people became more nomadic, moving between local areas in winter and summer. Among their descendents are the modern Timbisha Shoshone, who have lived in both Death Valley (*Tümpisa*) and the Panamint Valley (*Haütta*) since the 1400s.

The first Americans to find Death Valley were almost certainly the ill-fated 49ers, struggling to cross the desert to the gold fields with no map and no grasp of the terrain. The myths and misperceptions that surround them is unfortunate, because their journey is one of the great stories of the American West.

Like all other emigrants heading to the gold fields, the 49ers began their journey on the Oregon Trail, established in the 1830s and '40s as the only practical overland route through the Rockies. It began in St. Louis, where wagons could be transported west by steamship along the Missouri River. Where the river turned north, wagons disembarked at Independence and traveled in large parties through northeast Kansas to Grand Island, Nebraska; along the Platte River to Fort Laramie, Wyoming; through Idaho; to Portland, Oregon; and on to southwest Washington. It was more than 2,000 miles from one end to the other, and many emigrants, lacking money, horses or oxen, walked the entire length. By the time gold was discovered in 1848, the trail was so well established that it became the de facto route to California, splitting off near Salt Lake City.

In 1849, William Manly was, depending on the season, a trapper, woodcutter or laborer in and around Mineral Point, Wisconsin. He was 29 years old, a skilled tracker and marksman, and with his friend Asahel Bennett, often spent the winter months in the wild to trap marmot, mink, or beaver. Bennett was 35 and lived with his wife Sarah and three young children on a small farm in Mineral Point. When gold fever swept the country, Bennett decided to leave the farm and move his family to California. He invited his friend William Manly to join them.

In the early spring of 1849, the two men agreed to buy provisions separately and meet in St. Louis for departure. An undated letter from

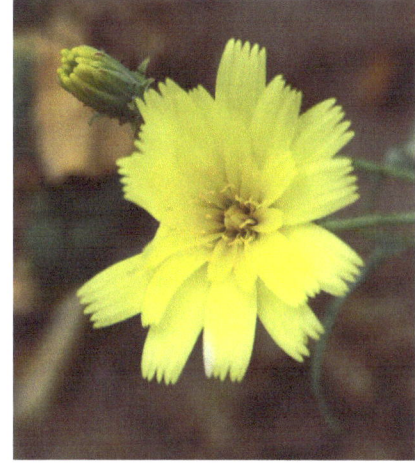

DESERT CHICORY
Chicory is a member of the sunflower family, a flower not usually associated with the desert.

Bennett caused Manly to miss their departure by two weeks. Manly set off alone, hoping to reunite with his friend somewhere along the trail. He had an extra woolen shirt, his rifle, and a few dollars in coin. He also brought a small supply of flour and bacon. His other supplies had been entrusted to the Bennetts.

Single men were not uncommon on the trail, and they often moved among the wagon trains as they traveled. They were welcome in any train as long as they were self-sufficient and caused no trouble. Manly had expected to travel with the Bennetts, who would be better provisioned with a wagon, and as he traveled alone he worried that he might not have enough money to survive the trip. He hired out as a teamster to a Charles Dallas in exchange for his board. Among the other teamsters was John Rogers, a 21-year-old blacksmith and butcher from Tennessee.

Manly found the trip at first to be uneventful. During the long days when he was not driving, he began to scout ahead of the wagons, to learn the geography of their position. The wagon train usually made 15 miles a day, a distance he could cover quite easily on foot.

"In the year 1850 the number of parties of emigrants bound to California from the Eastern States was so great that their trains of wagons formed what may be called almost a continuous procession from the Missouri River to Salt Lake City."

— John Spears,
Illustrated Sketches of Death Valley

By August his train had reached western Wyoming, and time was against the emigrants. The route to California split from the Oregon Trail at Sage, Utah. Those headed to the gold fields had to travel south to Salt Lake City, where they would restock and rest for the difficult journey across the arid Great Basin. From the Great Basin, the trail moved across the Sierra Nevada into California, and from there on to Sacramento. The Sierra could not be crossed past September, when heavy snows were expected to begin. It was the attempt to cross those mountains in fall that had doomed the Donner party only two years before, and the notorious outcome affected the journey of every wagon train that followed. Those who arrived in Salt Lake too late to cross the Sierra wintered over there until spring.

As the train approached Salt Lake, Manly and the other teamsters discovered that Dallas did not intend to board them during the winter stay. They also heard rumors that the Mormons in town would not hire outsiders for any work. With no job, no prospects and little money, the teamsters would have no way to pay for their stay through spring. Along with the train's cook, they quit Dallas to strike out on their own.

After a disastrous, nearly fatal attempt to reach California by sailing the Green River in impromptu canoes, the men split into groups and went in separate directions. Stranded, hungry and hopelessly lost, Manly's group was intercepted by friendly Utes. Chief Walker, a friend of Brigham Young, assumed that they were "Mormonee." He gave them food and showed them the safest trail back to Salt Lake.

Some 60 miles south of the city, Manly encountered another wagon train, and was overjoyed to find the Bennetts among its families. Wary of the fierce and clannish Mormons, Bennett told him, their train had departed from the Oregon Trail, determined to try an alternate route rather than winter in Salt Lake.

Ironically, they were following a Mormon captain named Jefferson Hunt, who was leading seven wagons across the Old Spanish Trail to San Bernardino, where the Mormons had a colony. Those going to the gold fields would follow Hunt to San Bernardino and then travel to Los Angeles and on to San Pedro, where they could board a ship for San Francisco. The alternate route would increase the distance they traveled, but would shorten the time it took them to get to Northern California. They had been camped for a brief time as they waited for the weather to cool enough to cross the desert to Los Angeles.

In September, after the wagon train began its long journey along the "southern route," another train lead by a Captain Smith overtook them. Smith claimed to have a map that showed an even shorter course around the Sierra. The "Walker shortcut" was said to utilize a mountain pass off the Old Spanish Trail to the Tulare valley. By using this map, they could save 500 miles by not going as far south as Los Angeles.

The emigrants were split on the decision. Hunt advised against the shortcut, but pledged that he would still guide those interested to San Bernardino. The two wagon trains, with a total of 107 wagons, proceeded west under Hunt and Smith until the trail split around present-day Enterprise, Utah. The majority of wagons elected to follow Captain Smith, and Hunt continued on the southern route without them. The Bennett family, accompanied by the Arcan family, the brothers John, Jacob and Henry Earhart, Manly and John Rogers, followed Smith.

Almost immediately, the Walker shortcut route proved difficult, if it existed at all. It was not clearly marked, difficult to traverse, and in most places was not wide enough for the wagons. Near what is now Beaver Wash, Utah, they encountered a canyon so deep that many wagons could not maneuver across. A number of families, shaken by the difficulty, turned around and left the train to rejoin the Hunt group on its much longer journey to Southern California.

Approximately 30 wagons continued on with Smith, but it was clear that the remaining journey would be treacherous. Unity and fellowship began to falter. The single men of the train declared that all families were on their own, and that they would not aid anyone who could not keep up during the journey. In his memoirs, Manly wrote that as the trip wore on and became more dangerous, he regretted not being able to flee the wagon train and travel more quickly on his own. He would remain loyal to the Bennetts even as he began to doubt their chances of survival.

As he had done on the Oregon Trail, Manly walked a day or two ahead, travelling alone and returning to report on what he had learned about the terrain. He borrowed Charlie Arcan's spyglass and began to climb to buttes and peaks to see greater distances. He was alarmed by the increasing barrenness of the land, and he determined that the group was traveling too far north, back in the direction of Salt Lake. He persisted in his objections to their route, and finally persuaded the group to turn west. By doing so they left the supposed Walker shortcut trail, and now followed no map at all. A group of men who had dubbed themselves the Jayhawkers broke off and continued to follow the shortcut trail north, but returned to the wagon train by the second night.

As he continued scouting, Manly realized that they were much farther from California than they had realized. He cited the emigrants' accepted belief that based on what they knew of John C. Fremont's travels, they had only to cross a single dry mountain range to find the green, fertile valley that ran all the way to the Pacific Ocean. What he saw instead were many mountains and the most desolate landscape he had ever seen. Any route to the north, south or east of them was impassable. A western route through the mountains was their only option.

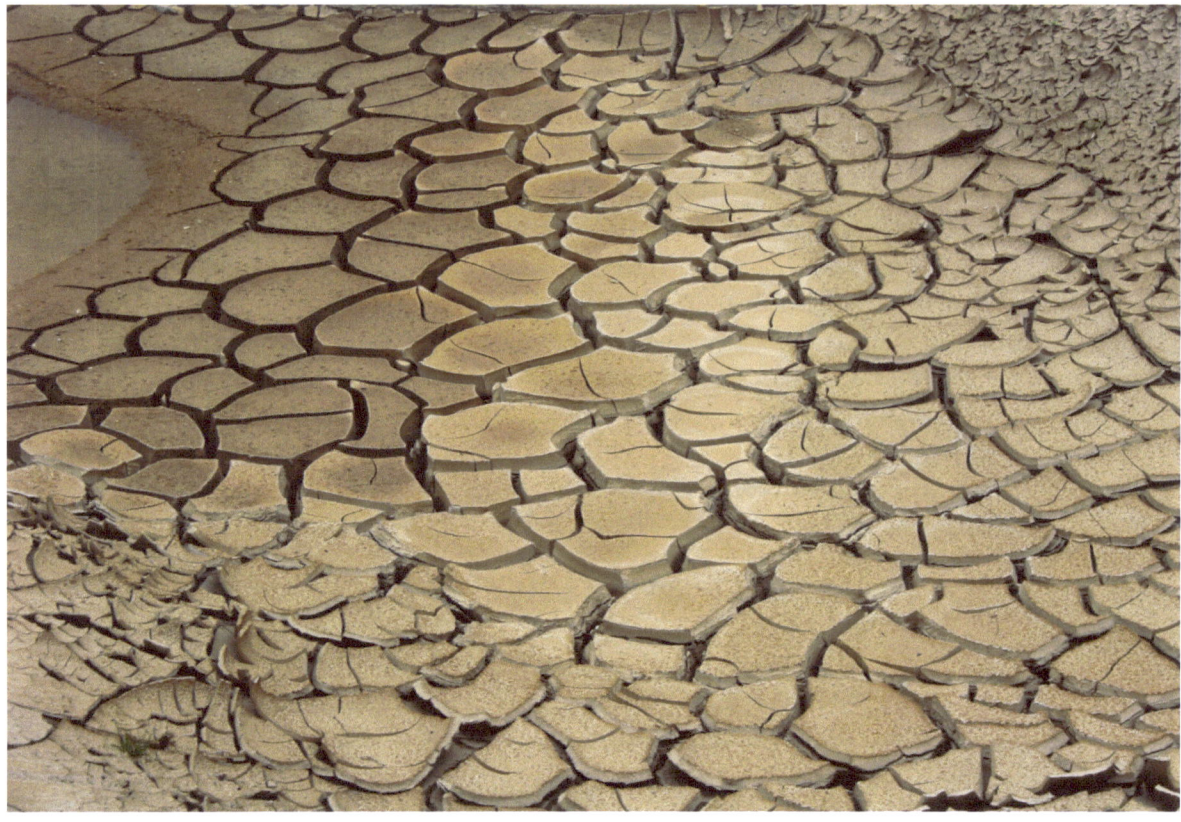

CRACKED EARTH
Death Valley has the highest evaporation rate in the United States—about 77 times the annual precipitation rate.

They had been driving toward a distant snowy peak that Manly believed had a pass that led into the gold fields. He called it Martin's Pass, and he estimated it was at least a month's hard journey away.

It was now late fall, about two months since they had left the Old Spanish Trail. As they slowly crossed what is now central Nevada, they faced a daily struggle to find enough water and enough grass for their oxen. On a good day, when they found a pool of water in a ravine, they saved it in large kegs. On most days, they found only dry lake beds. The oxen "suffered fearfully," Manly wrote, and grew gaunt. He continued to scout, and based on what he saw of the enormous salt flat lying ahead of them, privately considered their prospects hopeless.

Around what is now Groom Lake, the Jayhawkers again broke from the train and began the move across the flat, a journey Manly estimated would take them four to six days with no chance of finding water. He didn't expect them to survive. He persuaded the remaining group to detour from their western course to a mountain to the south. There was snow on its summit, and they were likely to find water at its base.

On the second night of their detour, Manly wrote that "a stray and crazy cloud" passed over them, leaving several inches of snow. At daybreak they found the starving, shivering oxen licking the snow for moisture. The small storm saved the wagon train—and the Jayhawkers to the north—from dying of thirst.

Despite the reprieve, the oxen were now so weak that the wagons were emptied to lighten their loads, and the emigrants reluctantly left everything behind except bedding and provisions. For some wagons, food supplies were exhausted, and those oxen about to die were slaughtered. The meat was poor, and the bone marrow was thick and streaked with blood. Nothing went to waste. The hides were made into moccasins to shoe the remaining foot-sore oxen.

In late December, they came to the area now known as Ash Meadows, just east of Death Valley. They found bitter, but drinkable water, and some grass for the oxen. As Manly continued to scout, he found the Jayhawkers' trail; they had survived the salt flat and had turned southward into Death Valley. The Bennetts, Arcans and the other wagons of their group had crossed into what is now Death Valley Junction.

On Christmas Day, Manly found the camp of Reverend J. Welsh Brier, whose family was the only one among the Jayhawkers. They had stopped alone at Furnace Creek while the others had gone ahead. Manly was startled to find the reverend lecturing his sons on the value of education, even as they were close to starvation.

He continued to walk north through the valley to the other Jayhawker camp near McLean Spring. The snowy peak the emigrants had followed for two months was now very close, and he enquired about Martin's Pass. The Jayhawkers responded that there was no pass, only another mountain range—the Panamints—and they believed they could continue on now only by foot. They had already killed their weakest oxen and burned their wagons to fuel fires to dry the meat. They equally divided the last teaspoons of rice and coffee among themselves. Each man was now on his own. Two men, Hamilton Fish and a Mr. Gould, walked out of camp together, confident that their long journey was nearly over.

Deeply discouraged, Manly made his way back to the Bennett-Arcan group. They had found a stream toward the southern end of the valley, and had made camp. Manly reported his belief that their only route out of the valley was to find a pass through the lower mountains to the south. But those mountains appeared dry and barren, and if they went that way they would struggle again to find enough water.

Moving south in the following days, they found a second spring that provided good water, but the next leg of their trip over a canyon was too rough for the wagons to cross. Bitterly disappointed, they had no choice but to return to the safety of the second spring.

Bennett made a desperate proposition: The wagon train would select the two strongest men left and send them on foot to find help. The others would remain in camp for 30 days awaiting their return. If they did not return in 30 days, the wagon train would consider them lost, and move on without them in search of escape.

Manly and John Rogers agreed to go. They were given new rawhide moccasins, knapsacks with the best of the camp's meager provisions, and they carried a rifle, two knives, and $30. They left 16 people in camp, including some children as young as two. If he and Rogers failed to return, Manly wrote, the others would last only as long as their oxen.

"Mrs. Bennett and Mrs. Arcan were in heart-rending distress. The four children were crying for water but there was not a drop to give them, and none could be reached before some time the next day. The mothers were nearly crazy, for they expected the children would choke with thirst and die in their arms, and would rather perish themselves than suffer the agony of seeing their little ones gasp and slowly die."

— **William Manly,**
Death Valley in '49

By nightfall the two men had climbed far up probably what is now called Manly Peak. They descended into the Panamint Valley and began the ascent up the next ridge. Manly realized they were following a Jayhawker trail, and they soon discovered the body of Hamilton Fish, who had left the Jayhawker's burned wagon camp two weeks before. They left his body as they found it; they had no tools and no suitable soil in which to bury him.

They traveled on without finding water, and became so dehydrated they couldn't chew the dried meat in their packs. To save energy they began to travel before daybreak. In the cold darkness they found a small patch of ice "not thicker than window glass," which they eagerly melted to drink. The ice saved their lives, much like the chance snowstorm had saved them near Groom Lake. Manly believed that if they had waited until daylight to travel, the patch would have melted and disappeared into the sand.

"There before us was a beautiful meadow of a thousand acres, green as a thick carpet of grass could make it, and shaded with oaks ... and over the broad acres of luxuriant grass was a herd of cattle numbering many hundreds, if not thousands ... All seemed happy and content, and such a scene of abundance and rich plenty and comfort bursting thus upon our eyes which for months had seen only the desolation and sadness of the desert was like ... a glimpse of Paradise."

— William Manly

After some days they spotted smoke, and following it, found the Jayhawkers in camp. There were water holes nearby, but many men were starving and some were reduced to eating ox hide. The Brier family, they told Manly, was somewhere behind them. Manly asked them about their route out of the valley, and learned where they had found water. They discussed the desert stretching out "like a small sea" that they still had to cross, and their utter hopelessness. As Manly and Rogers began to leave camp the next morning, several men asked them to notify their surviving relatives.

Later that day they came to a clearing of willows, where they found a good spring and a crude but abandoned corral. Farther on they came to a spot where they could see "peak after peak ... all of them white with snow," and what would later be called the Tehachapi pass—the southern end of the Sierra Nevada.

Rogers remembered hearing about such a pass on the trail from Salt Lake to Los Angeles, and eventually they found evidence of it. They followed it to a clean brook, and feasted on a quail, increasingly confident they were approaching "the promised land."

As they continued on the trail, the landscape slowly changed to grassy hills and cottonwoods. In mid-January, 1850, they crested the summit of a hill and looked down into a scene they could scarcely believe. It was a "beautiful meadow of a thousand acres," and a herd of cattle in the thousands, Manly wrote. They had stumbled across the Rancho San Francisquito, near the Tejon Pass.

They found a ranch adobe, but couldn't communicate with the Spanish-speaking vaqueros. They were directed to an American who was passing through the ranch on his way to the gold fields. He told them that they were 30 miles from Los Angeles, where they could get supplies.

Some 14 days had passed since they left the Bennett-Arcan group in Death Valley, and Manly worried that they would not be able to travel to Los Angeles and back to the valley within the 30 days agreed upon.

Sympathetic vaqueros lent them horses and escorted them to the Mission of San Fernando for the first part of their journey to Los Angeles. Near the mission they met a rancher named French, who arranged to provide them with the supplies necessary for their trip back. Los Angeles had been emptied by the gold rush, he told them.

With fresh provisions, three horses and a one-eyed mule, Rogers and Manly began the long trip back to Death Valley. They made their way to the willow corral, and to the water holes near where they had found the Jayhawkers in camp.

Manly retraced the trail the Jayhawkers had taken out of Death Valley, and by doing so knew where they had found water. Even so, the lack of grass and the arduous journey was hard on the horses, and they began to slow. Only the little mule carried on without difficulty.

Manly and Rogers visited the grave of William Isham, a Jayhawker who had died on the journey out of the valley, and they found again the unburied, undisturbed body of Hamilton Fish. Near the summit of the Argus range they left the Jayhawker trail to better accommodate the needs of the horses. The ascent was full of obstacles, and the horses were weak and worn out. Eventually the men could get them to go no farther, and feeling that time was too short, were forced to leave the horses behind.

When they came to a sheer precipice, they built the mule an inclined plane, and coaxed her across a ledge just four inches wide. Halfway across, with certain death below if she fell, the mule hesitated. To Manly, the moment "seemed to be weighed down with all the trials and hardships of many months … it seemed to be the time when helpless women and innocent children hung on the trembling balance between life and death." The mule made it safely across.

"Just as were passing out of sight the poor creatures neighed pitifully after us, and one who has never heard the last despairing, pleading neigh of a horse left to die can form no idea of its almost human appeal. We both burst into tears, but it was no use, [for] to try to save them we must run the danger of sacrificing ourselves, and the little party we were trying so hard to save."

— William Manly

Crossing the Panamint range and descending into Death Valley, they found the canyon when the Bennett-Arcan group had reluctantly turned around to return to the spring. They followed the wagon trail, and came across the body of the sea captain Richard Culverwell, one of the single men who had previously camped with the Jayhawkers.

The next day, the men returned to the camp they had left 26 days before. They learned that some of the others had left while they were gone, convinced that it was better to die in escape than to wait idly and perish. Bennett had begged them to stay, sure that Manly and Rogers would return. Among the last to leave was Captain Culverwell.

After the joyous reunion, Manly and Rogers told the remaining families how they crossed the desert, seen the snowy mountains, and found the green meadows of the ranch. They told them it was 250 miles to any livable part of California, and that they would not be able to take their wagons across the trail. They would have to walk.

The surviving oxen were still in poor shape but rested, and without wagons to pull, were crudely outfitted with harnesses made from wagon covers to serve as pack animals. Several of the children were severely malnourished, and others were too young to walk. A saddle was devised from a man's shirt so they could ride an ox.

Leaving with little more than the clothes they were wearing and a few tools for cooking, the emigrants began to walk out of the desert. It was now early February, 1850.

As they prepared to leave the valley for the leg through the Mojave Desert, Manly wrote, "we took off our hats, and then overlooking the scene of so much trial, suffering and death spoke the thought uppermost saying:—'Goodbye, Death Valley!'"

They still had a great deal of hardship ahead. It was a slow and physically demanding trip, and the women, weak and exhausted, fared worse than the men. More than once Mrs. Bennett sat on the ground and begged to be left alone to die. Manly and Rogers exhorted them on, encouraging them with reports of their progress or the promise of water and rest at the next camp.

When they reached the precipice where the little mule had been coaxed across, the men used ropes to hoist and lower the animals down. Manly and Rogers considered this their obstacle, and they had passed it without disaster. Once again they followed the Jayhawker trail, killing an ox when the meat ran out and struggling to find water. They, as well as the oxen, were hobbled by sore feet, and new moccasins were made from ox hide.

Eventually they made their way to Walker's Pass, the mountain shortcut they had tried to reach so many months before. They travelled to the camp where Manly and Rogers had found the Jayhawkers, and continued on to the willow corral. After several more days through the desert they finally came to the babbling brook that the two men had found near the ranch. "New life seemed to come to the dear women," Manly noted, and the oxen seemed as pleased as they were.

The 49ers finally reached Southern California in March, 1850, four months after they made their ill-fated turn from the Old Spanish Trail. They spent some days at Rancho San Francisquito, and began to go their separate ways.

William Manly went on to Los Angeles, where he briefly took a job at an inn opened by the Reverend J. Welsh Brier, whose family had survived the desert journey. He eventually made it to the gold fields, and after a reasonably successful stint at mining, decided to return to Wisconsin. He boarded a ship in San Francisco; walked across Panama; sailed a steamer to Cuba and continued to New Orleans; sailed up the Mississippi River to St. Louis; and finally walked home to Mineral Point. He wrote his memoirs, only to have them burn in a farmhouse fire. Ever the wanderer, he made the trip back to California via Panama soon after. In his later years he searched out Death Valley survivors and relatives, including Captain Culverwell's. He rewrote his memoirs, which were published in 1894. He died in Lodi, California, in 1903.

After his mining stint, John Rogers became a constable and farmer in Northern California. He died in Merced, California, in 1906.

The Arcans and the Bennetts left Rancho San Francisquito for San Pedro, where they boarded a ship for San Francisco. Asahel Bennett was reunited with Manly in the gold fields, where he sold goods to miners. Sarah Bennett died in 1857. Unable to care for his infant daughter, Asahel gave her to a childless couple who raised her. He remarried by 1870 and lived briefly in Utah. He died in Idaho in 1891.

Many of the Jayhawkers followed a path similar to that of Manly and Rogers to the Tejon Pass, and many of them survived their journey. One group went through the Sierra Nevada and made it to Owens Lake. They encountered snow and almost certainly would have perished if they had not been helped by Indians.

Another party of 11 Jayhawkers who left on foot before the burned wagon camp disappeared without a trace. Two of the men made it safely through to Owens Lake and eventually turned up in the gold fields. Several years later, the skeletons of the remaining nine men were found in the remains of another Death Valley camp.

The surviving Jayhawkers held annual reunions into the 1900s.

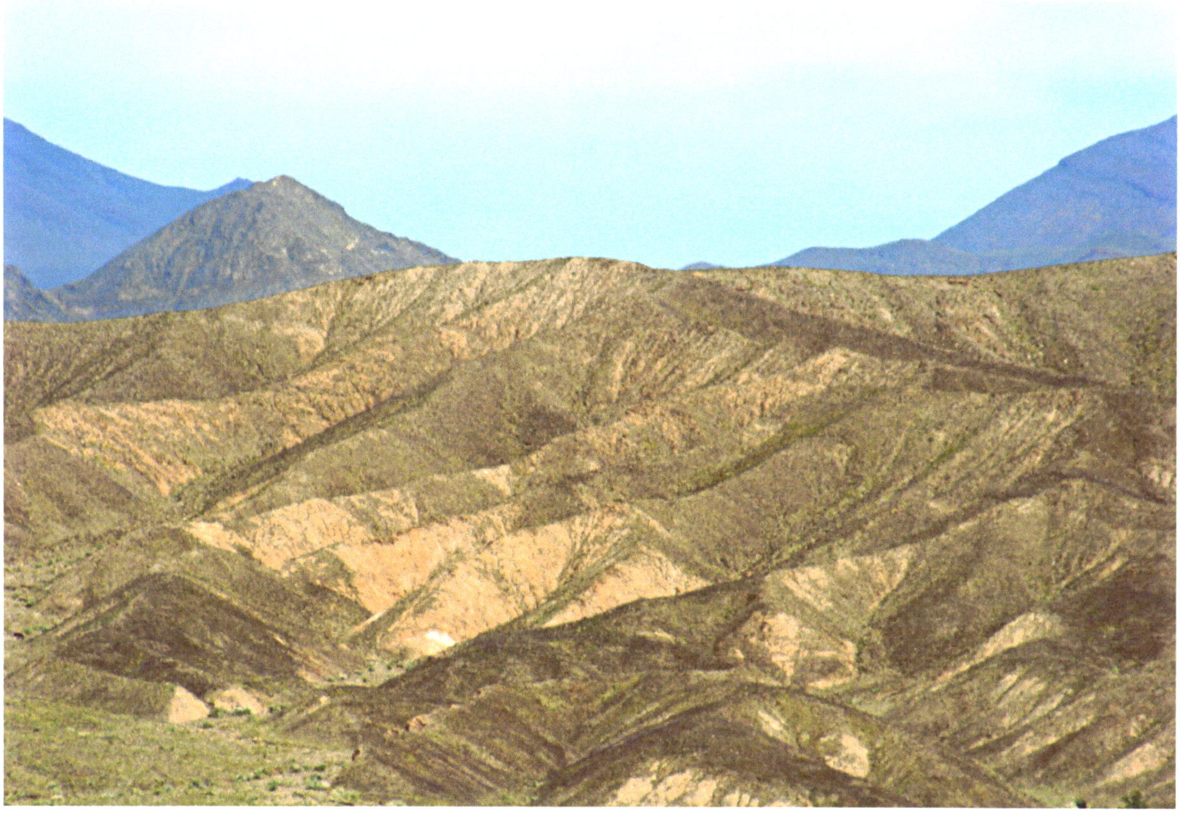

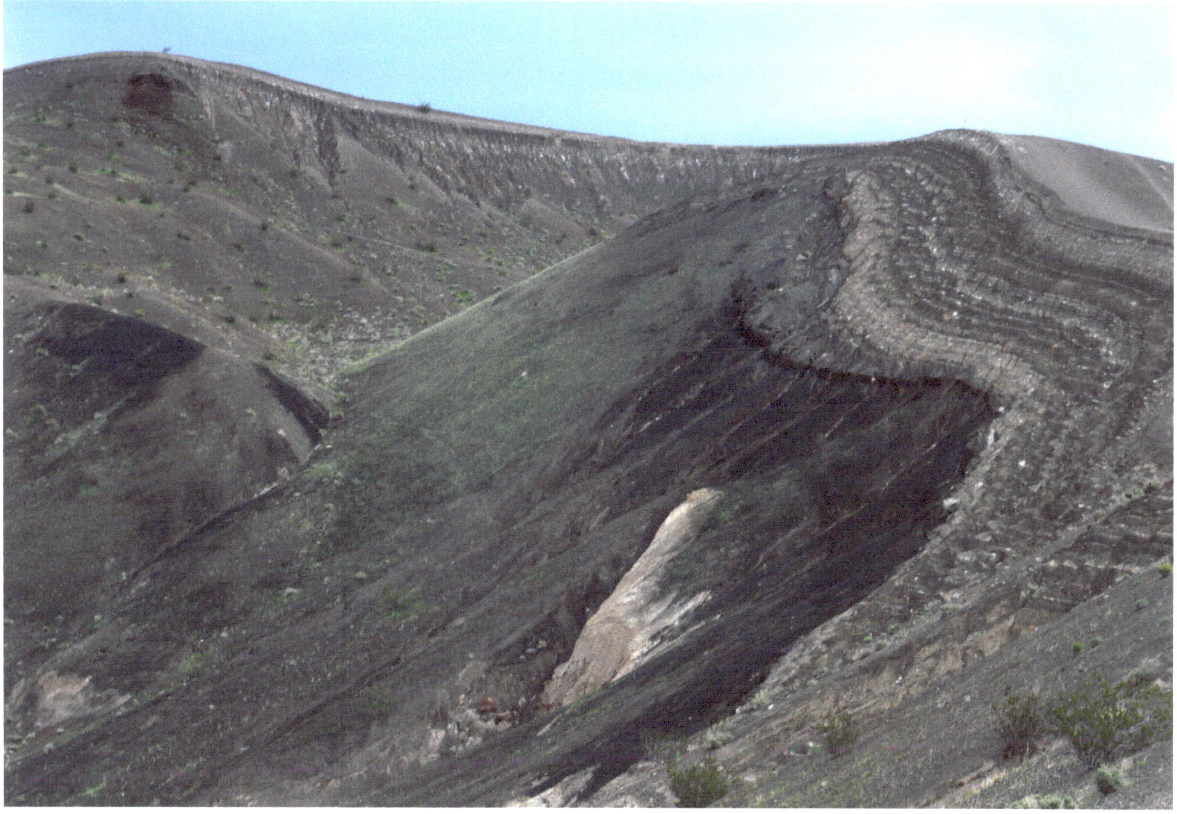

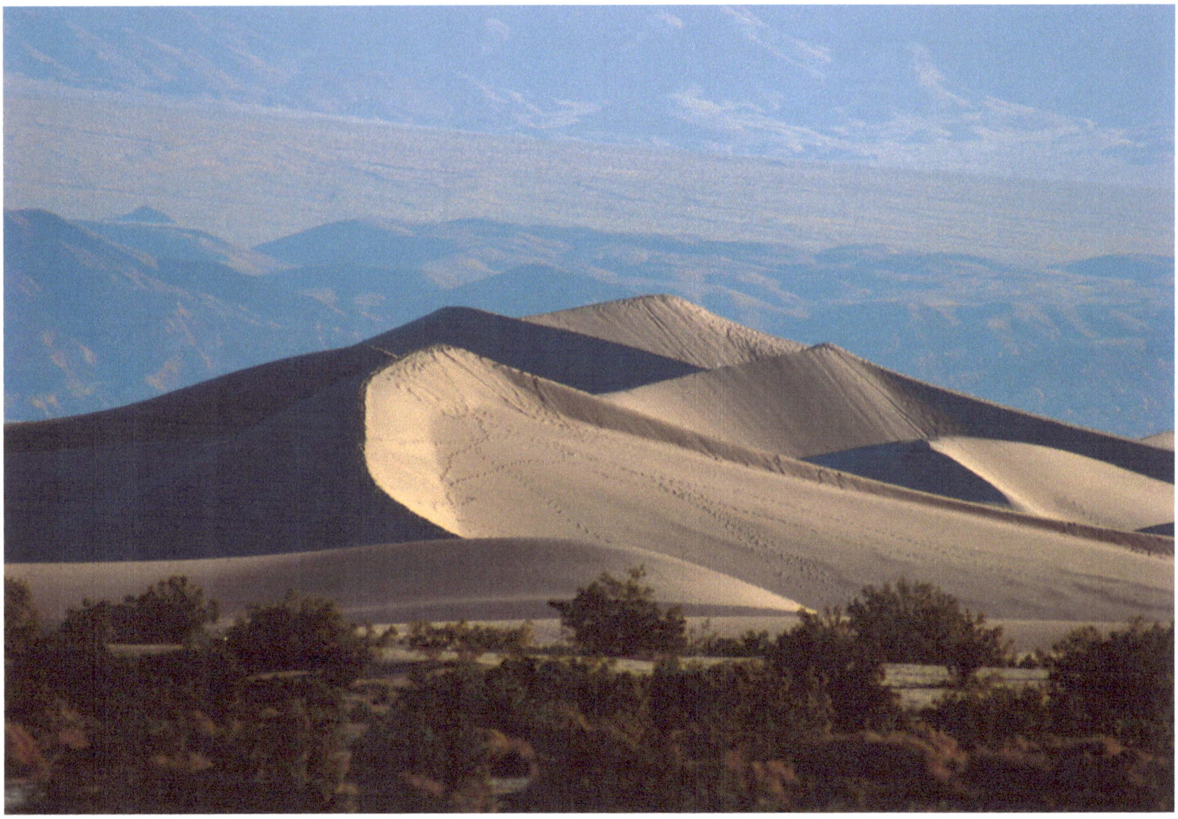

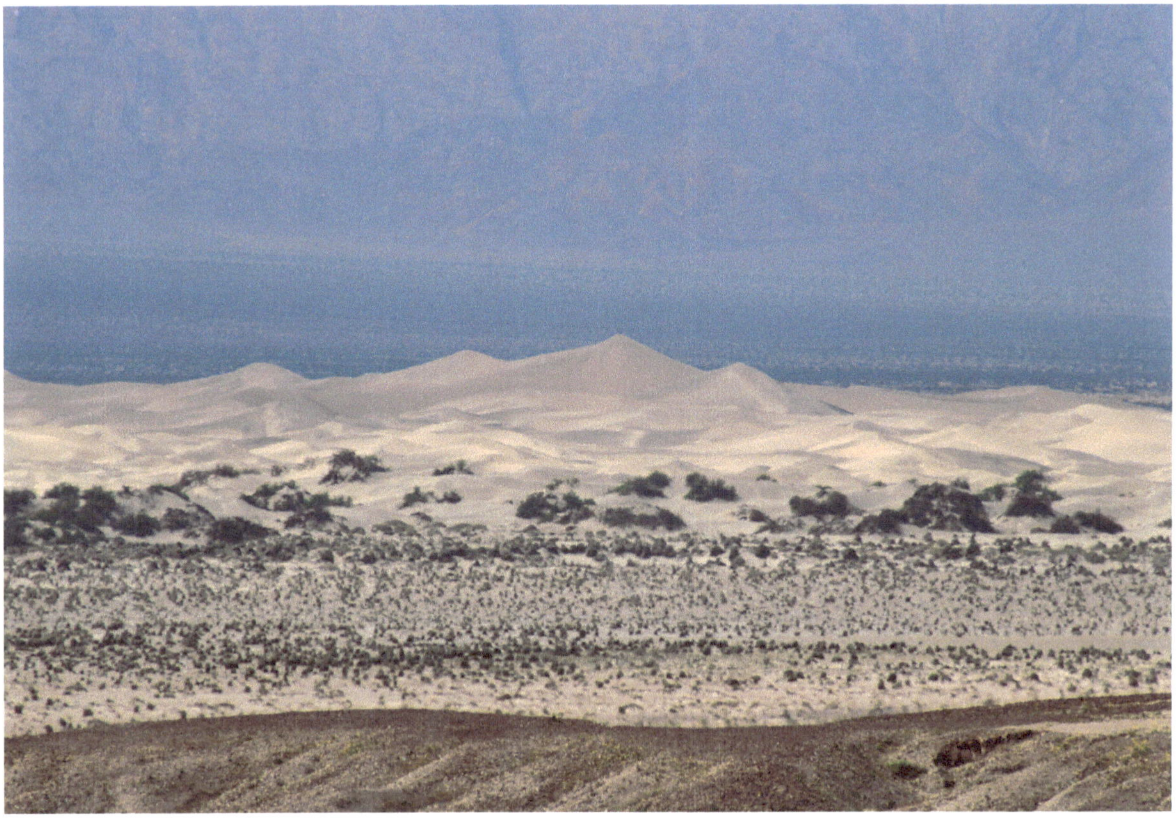

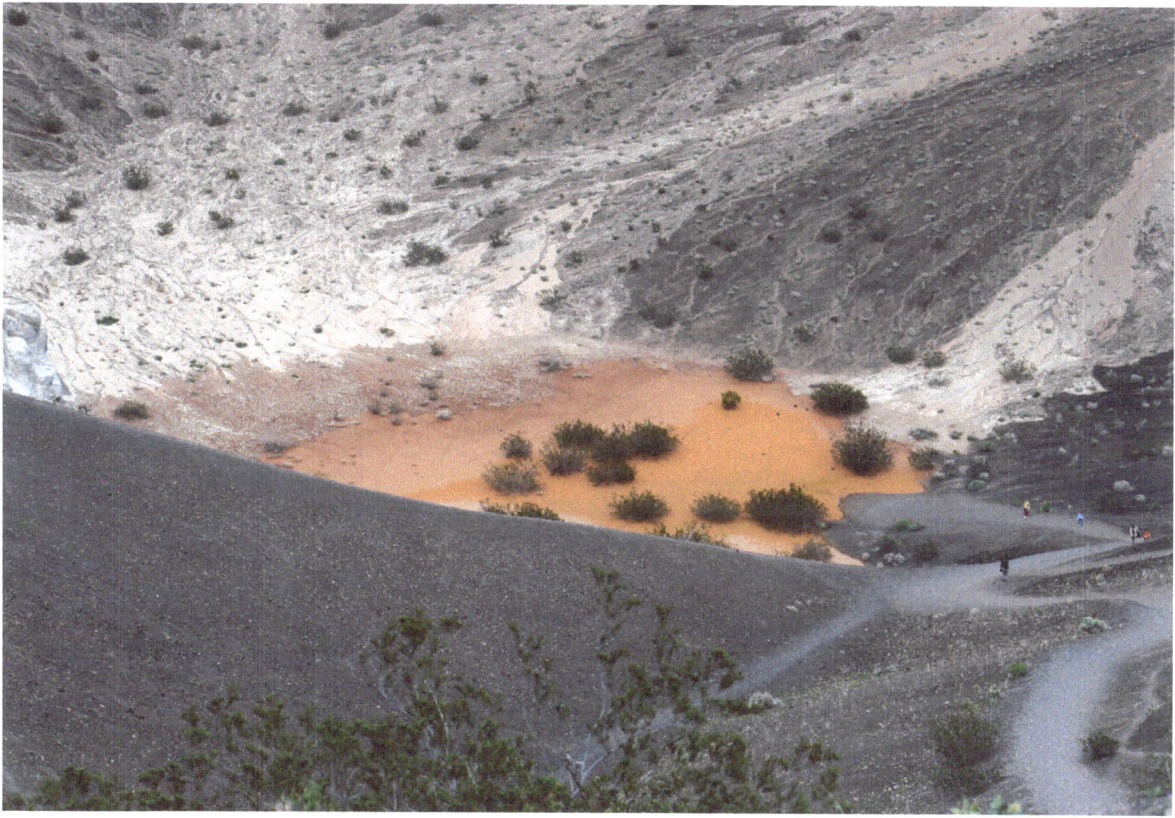

UBEHEBE CRATER
(top)
Located in the north valley, Ubehebe (an
Indian word for "Basket in the Rock")
is a volcanic crater that measures half a
mile wide and about 700 feet deep.

(opposite page)

THE DUNES
The Mesquite Flat Dunes, located near
Stovepipe Wells.

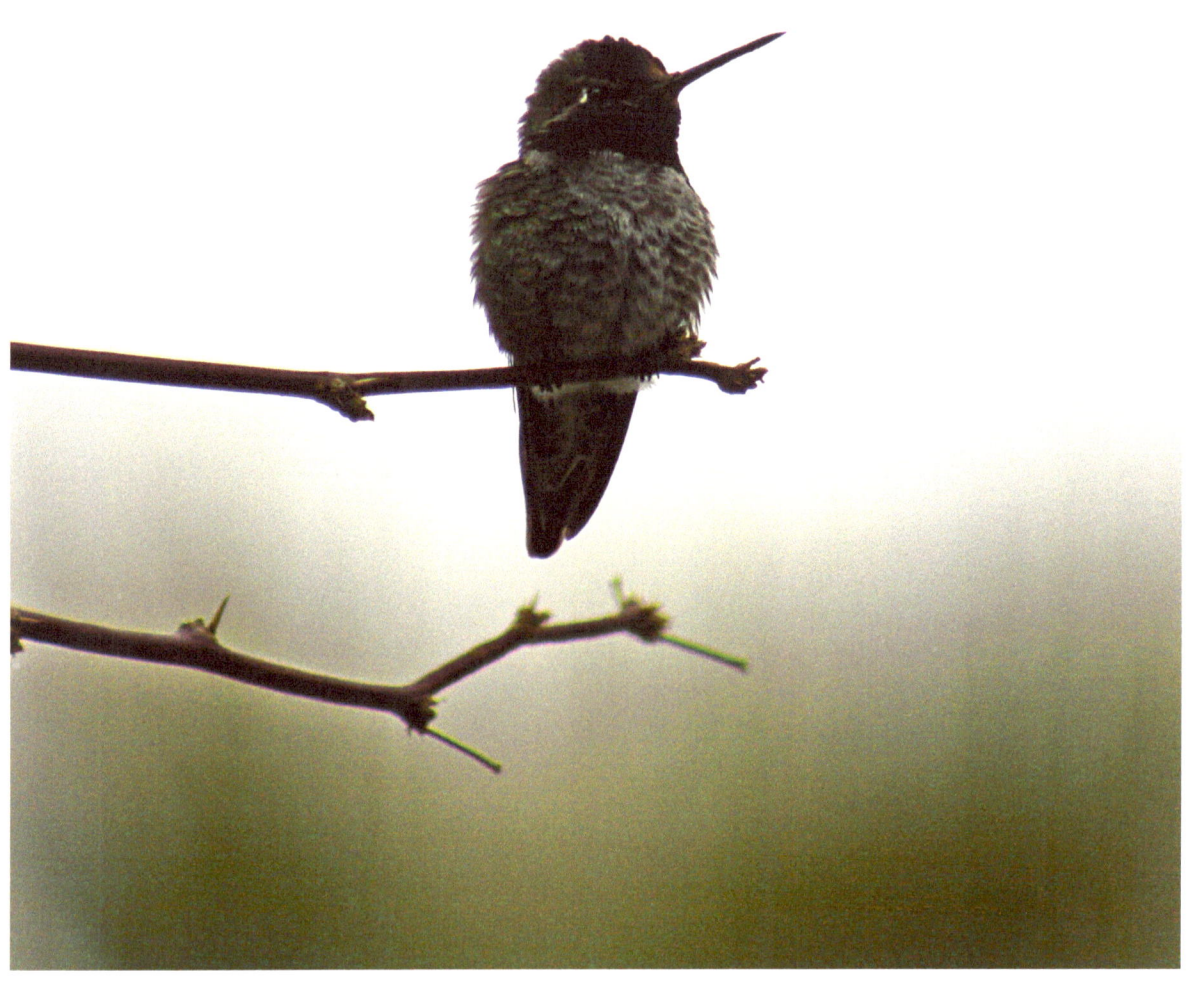

SCOTTY'S LOOKOUT
The wealth of wildflowers drew many birds to
Death Valley, especially near the gardens of
Scotty's Castle.

Boom and Bust

In the years that followed the California gold rush, a few prospectors drifted in and out of Death Valley in search of gold, silver or lead. A widely repeated story related how one of the 49ers had picked up a lead rock somewhere in the valley to use as part of a gun sight, and when he returned to civilization found it to be pure silver. As early as 1860, men set out to find the source of the famous "Gunsight lead." It never materialized.

There was a silver strike in 1873, and Panamint City boomed and busted by 1877. But it wasn't until borax was discovered in 1880 near Ash Meadows, just east of Death Valley, that the region experienced its longest mining boom.

At the time, borax was used chiefly for medicinal purposes, and was a relatively expensive commodity. There was already some borate mining in Teels' Marsh, Nevada, and in the Calico Mountains in San Bernardino County, but Death Valley was an opportunity for a much larger, and more lucrative, operation.

The raw material could be processed in the valley and shipped by wagon to Daggett, a rail spur near the Mojave Desert, where the borax would then be sent on to other destinations. But the lack of water and the steep route through the Panamints made using wagons inordinately difficult; there simply wasn't enough food or water between Death Valley and Daggett for horses or mules to endure the 10-day journey.

The solution was to build "freight trains"—wagons capable of carrying enormous amounts of borax plus spare food and water for a team and drivers. When finished, a single wagon stood about 12 feet high, and six feet across. Its back wheel was seven feet in diameter, and its bed was 16 feet long, four feet wide, and six feet deep. It weighed about 7,800 pounds unloaded, and could carry as much as 10 tons. When two wagons were coupled into a freight train, they could carry as much cargo as a rail car. A freight train required a team of 18 mules and two horses, a driver and a driver's assistant, known as a "swamper." The horses were harnessed to the first wagon; the mules were harnessed ahead of the horses, and the smartest and most obedient mules were always placed in the lead. When fully assembled, a freight train stretched out for more than a hundred feet.

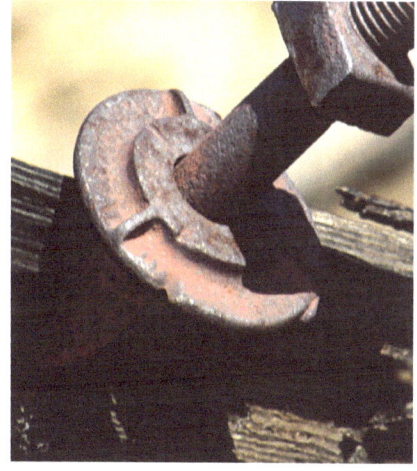

HISTORY INTACT
Extremely dry conditions in Death Valley preserve many of its mining ruins.

The teamster and his swamper had difficult and thankless jobs. Moving loaded freight trains and large teams up and down canyons and across salt roads was perilous, and it was not uncommon for a driver to be killed on a descent by a runaway train. There was a rigid 20-day schedule to follow, and only a half a day off between round trips.

The road between Death Valley and Daggett was divided into 10 stations, each an approximate day's distance from the next. Those "dry camps," stations that were not near natural water holes, were serviced by "wheeled water tanks" that brought water in from distant springs, as well as feed for the animals. But no amount of food and water allowed the freight trains to operate during the summer months; the heat was simply too much.

"The most important and valuable animal in the team is the 'nigh leader.' The swinging of the team in rounding curves, etc., depends greatly upon his doing his work intelligently. Each span of mules is attached to a set of single-trees and double-trees, that are hooked into the chain which extends from the leaders to the wagon. In going around a sharp curve, naturally this chain would be on a tangent from the leaders to the wagon[;] therefore, in order to keep the chain in this periphery of the curve, as well as the wagon in the road, it is necessary to have some of the spans of mules between the leaders and the wagon leap over the chain, and pull almost at right angles to the direction of the team, compelling them to step along 'sideways.' This they will do upon the driver shouting the command to them by name."

—Pacific Borax Company
The 20-Mule-Team &
Its Famous Driver Borax Bill

Another obstacle to borax mining was the lack of fuel needed to refine the raw material. Several types were imported at a great cost. Wagons brought in loads of "desert hay," or sagebrush, to burn in furnaces. Eventually, woodcutters were hired to cut down pine trees from the nearby mountains, while other men worked to dig up desert mesquite. When the need for fuel became desperate, one company began to freight in petroleum.

When borax was first discovered and processed in the United States in the 1850s, it sold for about 50 cents a pound, 47 cents of which was profit. Borax companies went to great lengths to exploit the reserves in and around Death Valley. So much of it was processed that it became a common household item, good as a cleaning agent, an antiseptic, a dentifrice; for curing meat, preventing sour milk, and fire-proofing plaster, among other uses.

Over time, the commodity price began to drop, from 50 cents a pound to eight cents a pound, and the high costs of fuel, labor and transportation made Death Valley less attractive as a mining site. The various borax works began to close, and the mines fell into ruin.

With the valley's industry on the wane, the Pacific Borax Company needed a return on investment in its Death Valley Railroad. It built the luxurious Furnace Creek Inn in 1927 to attract tourists to a place a newspaper had once called "hell without the inconveniences." It partially worked—Death Valley did become a destination for tourists, but they arrived by car, and the railroad closed in 1930.

In 1922, Chicago insurance man Albert Johnson and his wife Bessie began to build a vacation home in Death Valley. They used— and had trouble keeping—the finest craftsmen to build a mansion in the north valley. Their friend Walter Scott, an old-time miner and year-round valley resident, passed himself off as the owner of the home so often it became known as "Scotty's Castle." The stock market crash in 1929 kept Johnson from completely finishing construction.

After Herbert Hoover made Death Valley a national monument in 1933, the Civilian Conservation Corps began to build paved roads in and around the area. Mining officially ceased in the valley in the 1970s, and Death Valley became a National Park in 1994.

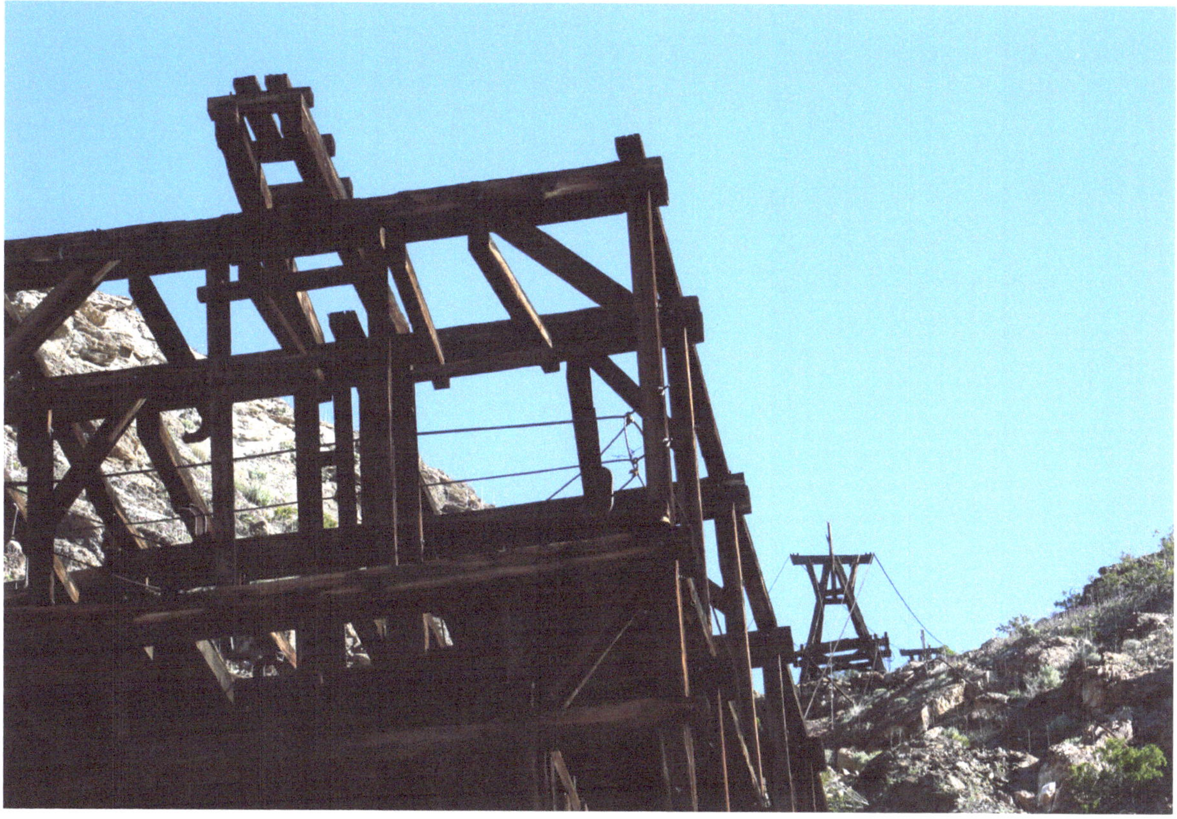

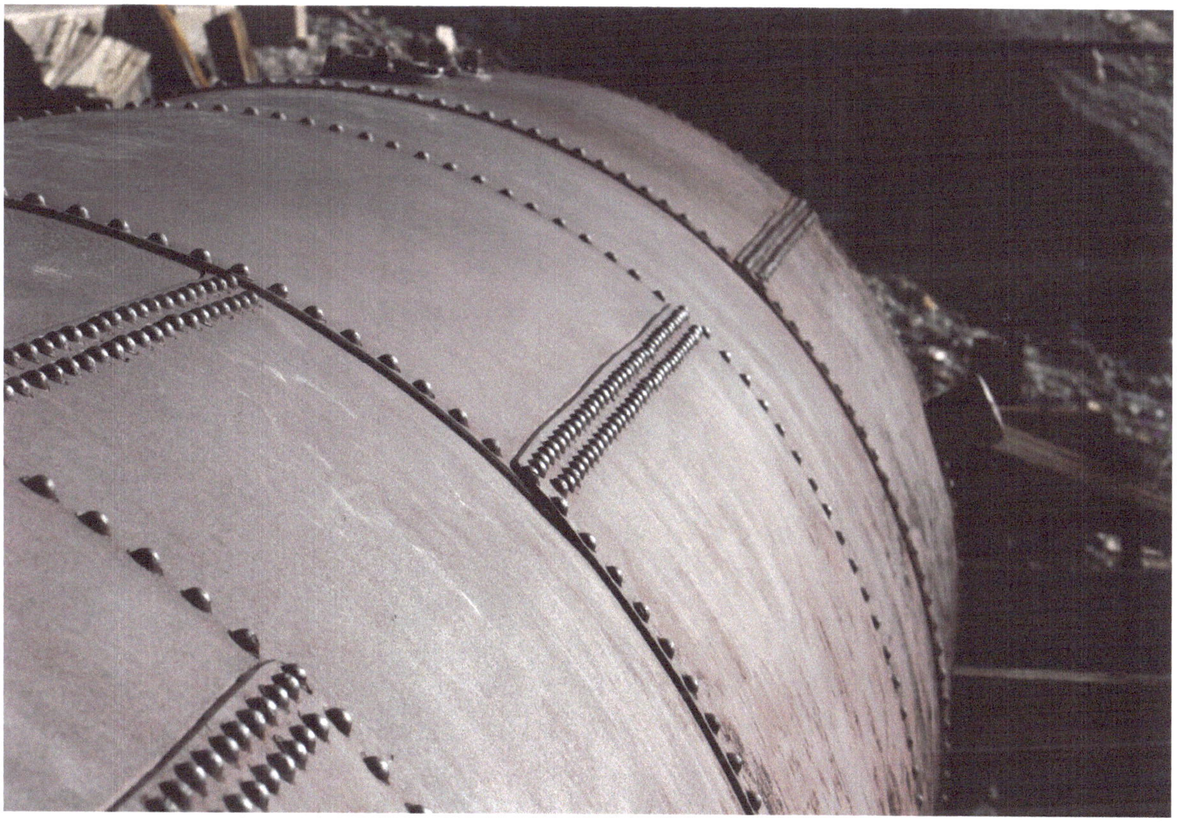

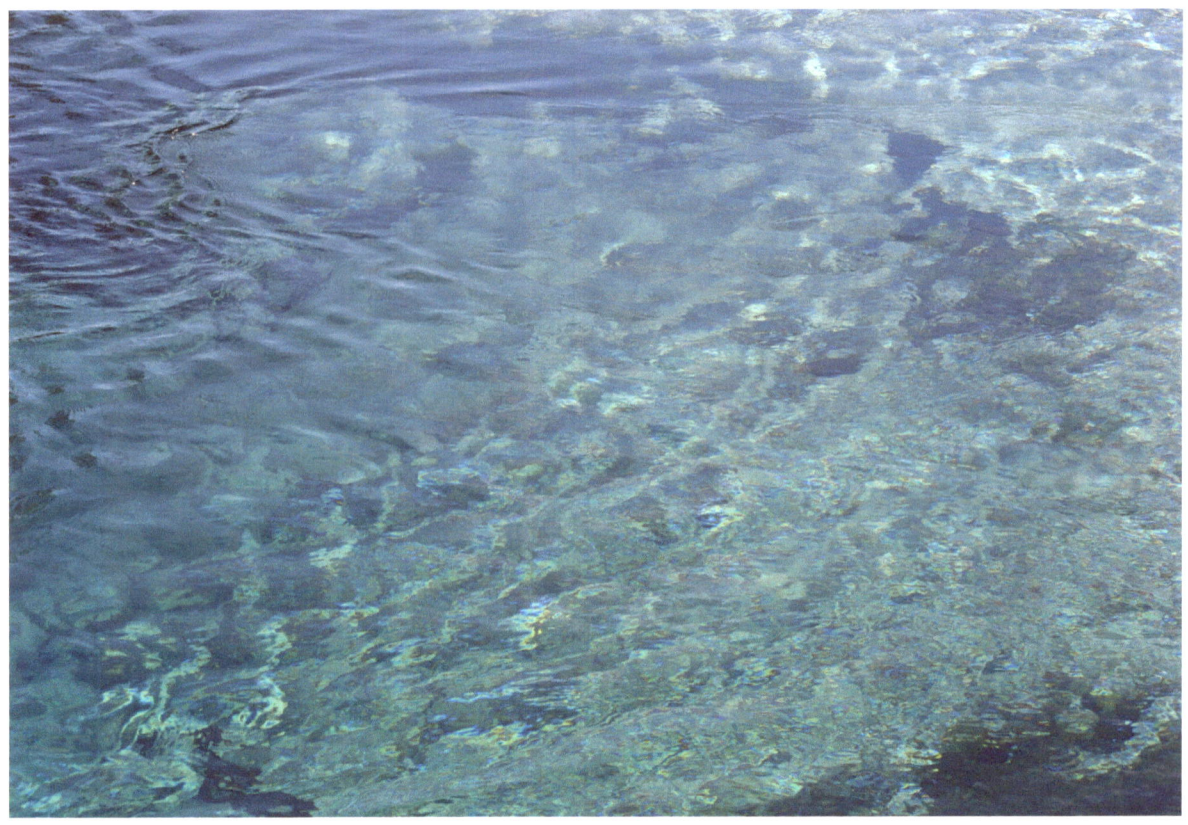

POND AT ASH MEADOWS
The Bennett party and the Jayhawkers
found fresh water and grass for their
oxen just east of Death Valley.

Bibliography

Calflora - Search for Plants. Web. 17 Dec. 2010.
<http://www.calflora.org/>.

"CalPhotos Plants: Common Names [D]." *CalPhotos.* Web. 17 Dec. 2010.
<http://calphotos.berkeley.edu/flora/com-D.html>.

The Famous Twenty Mule Borax Team from Death Valley California.
United States: Pacific Coast Borax, 19–. Print.

Hufford, David Andrew. *Death Valley Swamper Ike's Traditional Lore : Why, When, How?*
Los Angeles: D.A. Hufford, 1902. Print.

Manly, William Lewis. *Death Valley in '49. Important Chapter of California Pioneer History : the Autobiography of a Pioneer, Detailing His Life from a Humble Home in the Green Mountains to the Gold Mines of California : and Particularly Reciting the Sufferings of the Band of Men, Women and Children, Who Gave Death Valley Its Name.*
San Jose, CA: Pacific Tree and Vine, 1894. Print.

"NCDC: Climate of 2005: California Storms of Winter 2005." *NCDC: * National Climatic Data Center (NCDC) *.*
Web. 17 Dec. 2010.
<http://www.ncdc.noaa.gov/oa/climate/research/2005/california-storms2005.html>.

Spears, John Randolph. *Illustrated Sketches of Death Valley and Other Borax Deserts of the Pacific Coast.*
Chicago: Rand, McNally, 1892. Print.

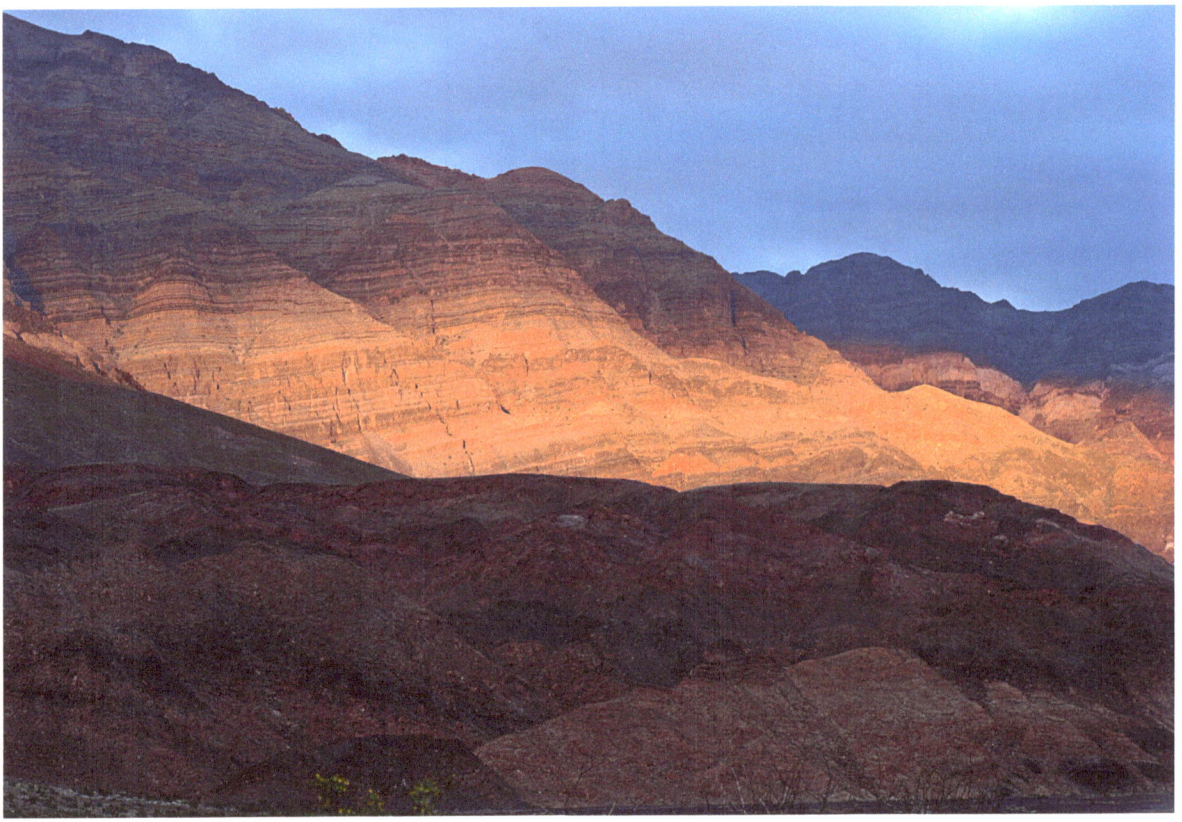

WINTER WARMTH
The last sunlight of the day highlights
the sediment layers of an ancient sea.

www.ingramcontent.com/pod-product-compliance
Lightning Source LLC
Chambersburg PA
CBHW041523280526

45792CB00004B/1351